Spiritual Energies in Daily Life

by

Rufus M. Jones

INTRODUCTION
RELIGION AS ENERGY

Religion is an experience which no definition exhausts. One writer with expert knowledge of anthropology tells us what it is, and we know as we read his account that, however true it may be as far as it goes, it yet leaves untouched much undiscovered territory. We turn next to the trained psychologist, who leads us "down the labyrinthine ways of our own mind" and tells us why the human race has always been seeking God and worshiping Him. We are thankful for his Ariadne thread which guides us within the maze, but we feel convinced that there are doors which he has not opened—"doors to which he had no key." The theologian, with great assurance and without "ifs and buts," offers us the answer to all mysteries and the solution of all problems, but when we have gone "up the hill all the way to the very top" with him, we find it a "homesick peak"—*Heimwehfluh* —and we still wonder over the real meaning of religion.

We are evidently dealing here with something like that drinking horn which the Norse God Thor tried to drain. He failed to do it because the horn which he assayed to empty debouched into the endless ocean, and therefore to drain the horn meant drinking the ocean dry. To probe religion down to the bottom means knowing "what God and man is." Each one of us, in his own tongue and in terms of his own field of knowledge, gives his partial word, his tiny glimpse of insight. But the returns are never all in. There is always more to say. "Man is incurably religious," that fine scholar, Auguste Sabatier, said. Yes, he is. It is often wild and erratic religion which we find, no doubt, but the hunger and thirst of the human soul are an indubitable fact. In different forms of speech we can all say with St. Augustine of Hippo: "Thou hast touched me and I am on fire for thy peace."

In saying that religion is energy I am only seizing one aspect of this great experience of the human heart. It is, however, I believe, an essential aspect. A religion that makes no difference to a person's life, a religion that *does* nothing, a religion that is utterly devoid of power, may for all practical purposes be treated as though it did not exist. The great experts—those who know from the inside what religion is—always make much of its dynamic power, its energizing and propulsive power. *Power* is a word often on the lips of Jesus; never used, it should be said, in the sense of extrinsic authority or the right to command and govern, but always in reference to an intrinsic and interior moral and spiritual energy of life. The kingdom of God comes with power, not because the Messiah is supplied with ten legions of angels and can sweep the Roman eagles back to the frontiers of the Holy Land, but it "comes with power" because it is a divine and life-transforming energy, working in the moral and spiritual nature of man, as the expanding yeast works in the flour or as the forces of life push the seed into germination and on into the successive stages toward the maturity of the full-grown plant and grain.

The little fellowship of followers and witnesses who formed the nucleus of the new-born Church felt themselves "endued with power" on the day of Pentecost. Something new and dynamic entered the consciousness of the feeble band and left them no longer feeble. There was an in-rushing, up-welling sense of invasion. They passed over from a visible Leader and Master to an invisible and inward Presence revealed to them as an unwonted energy. Ecstatic utterance, which seems to have followed, is not the all-important thing. The important thing is heightened moral quality, intensified fellowship, a fused and undying loyalty, an irresistible boldness in the face of danger and opposition, a fortification of spirit which nothing could break. This energy which came with their experience is what marks the event as an epoch.

St. Paul writes as though he were an expert in dynamics. "Dynamos," the Greek word for power, is one of his favorite words. He seems to have found out how to draw upon energies in the universe which nobody else had suspected were even there. It is a fundamental feature of his "Aegean gospel" that God is not self-contained but self-giving, that He circulates, as does the sun, as does the sea, and comes into us as an energy. This incoming energy he calls by many names: "The Spirit," "holy Spirit," "Christ," "the Spirit of Christ," "Christ in you," "God that worketh in us." Whatever his word or term is, he is always declaring, and he bases his testimony on experience, that God, as Christ reveals Him, is an active energy working with us and in us for the complete transformation of our fundamental nature and for *anewcr eation* in us.

All this perhaps sounds too grand and lofty, too remote and far away, to touch us with reality. We assume that it is for saints or apostles, but not for common everyday people like ourselves. Well, that is where we are wrong. The accounts which St. Paul gives of the energies of religion are not for his own sake, or for persons who are *bienné* and naturally saintly. They are for the rank and file of humans. In fact his Corinthian fellowship was raised by these energies out of the lowest stratum of society. The words which he uses to describe them are probably not over strong: "Be not deceived: neither fornicators, nor idolaters, nor adulterers, nor effeminate, nor abusers of themselves with mankind, nor thieves, nor covetous, nor drunkards, nor revilers, nor extortioners shall inherit the kingdom of God. *And such were some of you*: but ye are washed, but ye are sanctified, but ye are justified in the name [i.e. the power] of the Lord Jesus and by the Spirit of our God."[1]

It is to be noticed, further, that St. Paul does not confine his list of energies to those mighty spiritual forces which come down from above and work upon us from the outside. Much more often our attention is directed to energies which are potential within ourselves—even in the most ordinary of us—energies which work as silently as molecular forces or as "the capillary oozing of water," but which nevertheless are as reconstructive as the forces of springtime, following the winter's havoc. If the grace of God—the unlimited sacrificing love of God revealed in Christ—is for St. Paul the supreme spiritual energy of the universe, hardly less important is the simple human energy which meets that centrifugal energy and makes it operate within the sphere of the moral will. That dynamic energy, by which the man responds to God's upward pull and which makes all the difference, St. Paul calls faith.

We are so accustomed to the use of the word in a spurious sense that we are slow to apprehend the immense significance of this human energy which lies potentially within us. Unfortunately trained young folks and scientifically minded people are apt to shy away from the word and put themselves on the defensive, as though they were about to be asked to believe the impossible or the dubious or the unprovable. Faith in the sense in which St. Paul uses it does not mean *believing* something. It is a moral attitude and response of will to the character of God as He has been revealed in Christ. It is like the act which closes the electric circuit, which act at once releases power. The dynamic effect which follows the act is the best possible verification of the rationality of the act. So, too, faith as a moral response is no blind leap, no wild venture; it is an act which can be tested and verified by moral and spiritual effects, which are as real as the heat, light, and horse power of the dynamo.

Faith has come to be recognized as an energy in many spheres of life. We know what a stabilizer it is in the sphere of finance. Stocks and bonds and banks shift their values as faith in them rises or falls. *Morale* is only another name for faith. Our human relationships, our social structures, our enjoyment of one another, our satisfaction in books and in lectures rest upon faith and when that energy fails, collapses of the most serious sort follow. We might as well try to build a world without cohesion as to maintain society without the energy of faith.

We have many illustrations of the important part which faith plays in the sphere of physical health. The corpuscles of the blood and the molecules of the body are altered by it. The tension of the arteries and the efficiency of the digestive tract are affected by it. Nerves are in close sympathetic *rapport* with faith. It is never safe to tell a strong man that he is pale and that he looks ill. If two or three persons in succession give him a pessimistic account of his appearance, he will soon begin to have the condition which has been imagined. Dr. William McDougall gives the case of a boy who was being chased by a furious animal and under the impulse of the emergency he leaped a fence which he could never afterwards jump, even after long athletic training. The list of similar instances is a very long one. Every reader knows a case as impressive as the one I have given. The varieties of "shell-shock" have furnished volumes of illustrations of the energy of faith, its dynamic influence upon health and life and efficiency.

Faith in the sphere of religion works the greatest miracles of life that are ever worked. It makes the saint out of Magdalene, the heroic missionary and martyr out of Paul, the spiritual statesman of the ages out of Carthaginian Augustine, the illuminated leader of men out of Francis of Assisi, the maker of a new world epoch out of the nervously unstable monk Luther, the creator of a new type of spiritual society out of the untaught Leicestershire weaver, George Fox. Why do we not all experience the miracle and find *ther estofourselves* through faith? The main trouble is that we live victims of limiting inhibitions. We hold intellectual theories which keep back or check the outflow of the energy of faith. We have a nice system of thought which accounts for everything and explains everything and which leaves no place for faith. We know too much. We say to ourselves that only the ignorant and uncultured are led by faith. And this same wise man, who is too proud to have faith, holds all his inhibitory theories on a basis of faith! Every one of them starts out on faith, gathers standing ground by faith, and becomes a controlling force through faith!

There are many other spiritual energies, some of which will be dealt with specifically or implicitly in the later chapters of this book. Not often in the history of the modern world certainly have spiritual energies seemed more urgently needed than to-day. Our troubles consist largely now of failure to lay hold of moral and spiritual forces that lie near at hand and to utilize powers that are within our easy reach. Our stock of faith and hope and love has run low and we realize only feebly what mighty energies they can be.

I hope that these short essays may help in some slight way to indicate that the ancient realities by which men live still abide, and that the invisible energies of the spirit are real, as they have always been real. We have had an impressive demonstration that a civilization built on external force and measured in terms of economic achievements cannot stand its ground and is unable to speak to the condition of persons endowed and equipped as we are. We are bound to build a higher civilization, to create a greater culture, and to form a truer kingdom of life or we must write "*Mene*" on all human undertakings. That is our task now, and it is a serious one for which we shall need all the energies that the universe puts at our disposal. I am told that when the great Hellgate bridge was being built over the East River in New York the engineers came upon an old derelict ship, lying embedded in the river mud, just where one of the central piers of the bridge was to go down through to its bedrock foundation. No tug boat could be found that was able to start the derelict from its ancient bed in the ooze. It would not move, no matter what force was applied. Finally, with a sudden inspiration one of the workers hit upon this scheme. He took a large flat-boat, which had been used to bring stone down the river, and he chained it to the old sunken ship when the tide was low. Then he waited for the great tidal energies to do their work. Slowly the rising tide, with all the forces of the ocean behind it and the moon above it, came up under the flat-boat, raising it inch by inch. And as it came up, lifted by irresistible power, the derelict came up with it, until it was entirely out of the mud that had held it. Then the boat, with its subterranean load, was towed out to sea where the old waterlogged ship was unchained and allowed to drop forever out of sight and reach.

There are greater forces than those tidal energies waiting for us to use for our tasks. They have always been there. They are there now. But they do not *work*, they do not *operate*, until we lay hold of them and use them for our present purposes. We must be *co-workerswithGod* .

Haverford, Pennsylvania.

Mid Winter, 1922.

CONTENTS

	PAGE
INTRODUCTION: RELIGION AS ENERGY	vii

CHAPTER I
THE CENTRAL PEACE

I. Peace That Passes Understanding	1
II. The Search for a Refuge	5
III. What We Want Most	10

CHAPTER II
THE GREAT ENERGIES THAT WORK

I. Trying the Better Way	15
II. He Came to Himself	23
III. Some New Reasons for "Loving Enemies"	29

CHAPTER III
THE POWER THAT WORKETH IN US

I. Where the Beyond Breaks Through	35
II. Conquering by an Inner Force	41
III. Living in the Presence of the Eternal	46

CHAPTER IV
THE WAY OF VISION

I. Days of Greater Visibility	50
II. The Prophet and His Tragedies	54
III. A Long Distance Call	60

CHAPTER V
THE WAY OF PERSONALITY

I. Another Kind of Hero	65
II. The Better Possession	69
III. The Greatest Rivalries of Life	74

CHAPTER VI
AGENCIES OF CONSTRUCTION

I. THE CHURCH OF THE LIVING GOD	79
II. THE NURSERY OF SPIRITUAL LIFE	83
III. THE DEMOCRACY WE AIM AT	86
IV. THE ESSENTIAL TRUTH OF CHRISTIANITY	91

CHAPTER VII
THE NEAR AND THE FAR

I. THINGS PRESENT AND THINGS TO COME	98
II. TWO TYPES OF MINISTRY	102
III. WE HAVE SEEN HIS STAR	106

CHAPTER VIII
THE LIGHT-FRINGED MYSTERY

I. THE RELIGIOUS SIGNIFICANCE OF DEATH	111
II. THE NEW BORN OUT OF THE OLD	127

CHAPTER IX
THE MYSTIC'S EXPERIENCE OF GOD   133

CHAPTER X
PSYCHOLOGY AND THE SPIRITUAL LIFE   160

CHAPTER I
THE CENTRAL PEACE

I
PEACE THAT PASSES UNDERSTANDING

We are all familiar with the coming of a peace into our life at the terminus of some great strain or after we have weathered a staggering crisis. When a long-continued pain which has racked our nerves passes away and leaves us free, we suddenly come into a zone of peace. When we have been watching by a bedside where a life, unspeakably precious to us, has lain in the grip of some terrible disease and at length successfully passes the crisis, we walk out into the fields under the altered sky and feel a peace settle down upon us, which makes the whole world look different. Or, again, we have been facing some threatening catastrophe which seemed likely to break in on our life and perhaps end forever the calm and even tenor of it, and just when the hour of danger seemed darkest and our fear was at its height, some sudden turn of things has brought a happy shift of events, the danger has passed, and a great peace has come over us instead of the threatened trouble. In all these cases the peace which succeeds pain and strain and anxiety is a thoroughly natural, reasonable peace, a peace which comes in normal sequence and is quite accessible to the understanding. We should be surprised and should need an explanation if we heard of an instance of a passing pain or a yielding strain that was not followed by a corresponding sense of peace. One who has seen a child that was lost in a crowded city suddenly find his mother and find safety in her dear arms has seen a good case of this sequential peace, this peace which the understanding can grasp and comprehend. We behold it and say, "How otherwise!"

There is, St. Paul reminds us, another kind of peace of quite a different order. It baffles the understanding and transcends its categories. It is a peace which comes, not after the pain is relieved, not after the crisis has passed, not after the danger has disappeared; but in the midst of the pain, while the crisis is still on, and even in the imminent presence of the danger. It is a peace that is not banished or destroyed by the frustrations which beset our lives; rather it is in and through the frustrations that we first come upon it and enter into it, as, to use St. Paul's phrase, into a garrison which guards our hearts and minds.

Each tested soul has to meet its own peculiar frustrations. All of us who work for "causes" or who take up any great piece of moral or spiritual service in the world know more about defeats and disappointments than we do about success and triumphs. We have to learn to be patient and long-suffering. We must become accustomed to postponements and delays, and sometimes we see the work of almost a lifetime suddenly fail of its end. Some turn of events upsets all our noble plans and frustrates the result, just when it appeared ready to arrive. Death falls like lightning on a home that had always before seemed sheltered and protected, and instantly life is profoundly altered for those who are left behind. Nothing can make up for the loss. There is no substitute for what is gone. The accounts will not balance; frustration in another form confronts us. Or it may be a breakdown of physical or mental powers, or peradventure both together, just when the emergencies of the world called for added energy and increased range of power from us. The need is plain, the harvest is ripe, but the worker's hand fails and he must contract when he would most expand. Frustration looks him straight in the face. Well, to achieve a peace under those circumstances is to have a peace which does not follow a normal sequence. It is not what the world expects. It does not accord with the ways of thought and reasoning. It passes all understanding. It brings another kind of world into operation and reveals a play of invisible forces upon which the understanding had not reckoned. In fact, this strange intellect-transcending peace, in the very midst of storm and strain and trial, is one of the surest evidences there is of God. One may in his own humble nerve-power succeed in acquiring a stoic resignation so that he can say,

> "In the fell clutch of circumstance
>   I have not winced nor cried aloud.
> Under the bludgeonings of chance
>   My head is bloody, but unbowed."

He may, by sheer force of will, keep down the lid upon his emotions and go on so nearly unmoved that his fellows can hear no groan and will wonder at the way he stands the universe. But peace in the soul is another matter. To have the whole heart and mind garrisoned with peace even in Nero's dungeon, when the imperial death sentence brings frustration to all plans and a terminus to all spiritual work, calls for some world-transcending assistance to the human spirit. Such peace is explained only when we discover that it is "the peace of God," and that it came because the soul broke through the ebbings and flowings of time and space and allied itself with the Eternal.

II
THE SEARCH FOR A REFUGE

Few things are more impressive than the persistent search which men have made in all ages for a refuge against the dangers and the ills that beset life. The cave-men, the cliff-dwellers, the primitive builders of shelters in inaccessible tree tops, are early examples of the search for human defenses against fear. Civilization slowly perfected methods of refuge and defense of elaborate types, which, in turn, had to compete with ever-increasing ingenuity of attack and assault. But I am not concerned here with these material strongholds of refuge and defense. I am thinking rather of the human search for shelter against other weapons than those which kill the body. We are all trying, in one way or another, to discover how to escape from "the heavy and weary weight of all this unintelligible world," how to bear the slings and arrows of outrageous fortune. We are sensitively constructed, with nerves exposed to easy attack. We are all shelterless at some point to the storms of the world. Even the most perfectly equipped and impervious heroes prove to be vulnerable at some one uncovered spot. Sooner or later our protections fail, and the pitiless enemies of our happiness get through the defenses and reach the quick and sensitive soul within us. How to rebuild our refuge, how to find real shelter, is our problem. What fortress is there in which the soul is safe from fear and trouble?

The most common expedient is one which will drug the sensitive nerves and produce an easy relief from strain and worry. There is a magic in alcohol and kindred distillations, which, like Aladdin's genie, builds a palace of joy and, for the moment, banishes the enemy of all peace. The refuge seems complete. All fear is gone, worry is a thing of the past. The jargon of life is over, the pitiless problem of good and evil drops out of consciousness. The shelterless soul seems covered and housed. Intoxication is only one of the many quick expedients. It is always possible to retreat from the edge of strenuous battle into some one of the many natural instincts as a way of refuge. The great instinctive emotions are absorbing, and tend to obliterate everything else. They occupy the entire stage of the inner drama, and push all other actors away from the footlights of consciousness, so that here, too, the enemies of peace and joy seem vanquished, and the refuge appears to be found.

That multitudes accept these easy ways of defense against the ills of life is only too obvious. The medieval barons who could build themselves castles of safety were few in number. Visible refuges in any case are rare and scarce, but the escape from the burdens and defeats of the world in drink and drug and thrilling instinctive emotion is, without much difficulty, open to every man and within easy reach for rich and poor alike, and many there be that seize upon this method. The trouble with it is that it is a very temporary refuge. It works, if at all, only for a brief span. It plays havoc in the future with those who resort to it. It rolls up new liabilities to the ills one would escape. It involves far too great a price for the tiny respite gained. And, most of all, it discounts or fails to reckon with the inherent greatness of the human soul. We are fashioned for stupendous issues. Our very sense of failure and defeat comes from a touch of the infinite in our being. We look before and after, and sigh for that which is not, just because we can not be contented with finite fragments of time and space. We are meant for greater things than these trivial ones which so often get our attention and absorb us; but the moment the soul comes to itself, its reach goes beyond the grasp, and it feels an indescribable discontent and longing for that for which it was made. To seek refuge, therefore, in some narcotic joy, to still the onward yearning of the soul by drowning consciousness, to banish the pain of pursuit by a barbaric surge of emotions, is to strike against the noblest trait of our spiritual structure; it means committing suicide of the soul. It cannot be a real man's way of relief.

In fact, nothing short of finding the goal and object for which the soul, the spiritual nature in us, is fitted will ever do for beings like us. St. Augustine, in words of immortal beauty, has said that God has made us for himself, and our hearts are restless until we rest in him. It is not a theory of poet or theologian. It is a simple fact of life, as veritable as the human necessity for food. There is no other shelter for the soul, no other refuge or fortress will ever do for us but God. "We tremble and we burn. We tremble, knowing that we are unlike him. We burn, feeling that we are like him."

In hours of loss and sorrow, when the spurious props fail us, we are more apt to find our way back to the real refuge. We are suddenly made aware of our shelterless condition, alone, and in our own strength. Our stoic armor and our brave defenses of pride become utterly inadequate. We are thrown back on reality. We have then our moments of sincerity and insight. We feel that we cannot live without resources from beyond our own domain. We must have God. It is then, when one knows that nothing else whatever will do, that the great discovery is made. Again and again the psalms announce this. When the world has caved in; when the last extremity has been reached; when the billows and water-spouts of fortune have done their worst, you hear the calm, heroic voice of the lonely man saying: "God is our refuge and fortress, therefore will not we fear though the earth be removed, though the mountains be carried into the midst of the sea." That is great experience, but it is not reserved for psalmists and rare patriarchs like Job. It is a privilege for common mortals like us who struggle and agonize and feel the thorn in the flesh, and the bitter tragedy of life unhealed. Whether we make the discovery or not, God is there with us in the furnace. Only it makes all the difference if we do find him as the one high tower where refuge is not for the passing moment only, but is an eternal attainment.

III
WHAT WE WANT MOST

There are many things which we want—things for which we struggle hard and toil painfully. Like the little child with his printed list for Santa Claus, we have our list, longer or shorter, of precious things which we hope to see brought within our reach before we are gathered to our fathers. The difference is that the child is satisfied if he gets one thing which is on his list. We want everything on ours. The world is full of hurry and rush, push and scramble, each man bent on winning some one of his many goals. But, in spite of this excessive effort to secure the tangible goods of the earth, it is nevertheless true that deep down in the heart most men want the peace of God. If you have an opportunity to work your way into that secret place where a man really lives, you will find that he knows perfectly well that he is missing something. This feeling of unrest and disquiet gets smothered for long periods in the mass of other aims, and some men hardly know that they have such a thing as an immortal soul hidden away within. But, even so, it will not remain quiet. It cries out like the lost child who misses his home. When the hard games of life prove losing ones, when the stupidity of striving so fiercely for such bubbles comes over him, when a hand from the dark catches away the best earthly comfort he had, when the genuine realities of life assert themselves over sense, he wakes up to find himself hungry and thirsty for something which no one of his earthly pursuits has supplied or can supply. He wants God. He wants peace. He wants to feel his life founded on an absolute reality. He wants to have the same sort of peace and quiet steal over him which used to come when as a child he ran to his mother and had all the ills of life banished from thought in the warm love of her embrace.

But it is not only the driving, pushing man, ambitious for wealth and position, who misses the best thing there is to get—the peace of God. Many persons who are directly seeking it miss it. Here is a man who hopes to find it by solving all his difficult intellectual problems. When he can answer the hard questions which life puts to him, and read the riddles which the ages have left unread, he thinks his soul will feel the peace of God. Not so, because each problem opens into a dozen more. It is a noble undertaking to help read the riddles of the universe, but let no one expect to enter into the peace of God by such a path. Here is another person who devotes herself to nothing but to seeking the peace of God. Will she not find it? Not that way. It is not found when it is sought for its own sake. He or she who is living to get the joy of divine peace, who would "have no joy but calm," will probably never have the peace which passeth understanding. Like all the great blessings, it comes as a by-product when one is seeking something else. Christ's peace came to him not because he sought it, but because he accepted the divine will which led to Gethsemane and Calvary. Paul's peace did not flow over him while he was in Arabia seeking it, but while he was in Nero's prison, whither the path of his labors for helping men had led him. He who forgets himself in loving devotion, he who turns aside from his self-seeking aims to carry joy into any life, he who sets about doing any task for the love of God, has found the only possible road to the permanent peace of God.

There are no doubt a great many persons working for the good of others and for the betterment of the world who yet do not succeed in securing the peace of God. They are in a frequent state of nerves; they are busy here and there, rushing about perplexed and weary, fussy and irritable. With all their efforts to promote good causes, they do not quite attain the poise and calm of interior peace. They are like the tumultuous surface of the ocean with its combers and its spray, and they seldom know the deep quiet like that of the underlying, submerged waters far below the surface. The trouble with them is that they are carrying themselves all the time. They do not forget themselves in their aims of service. They are like the ill person who is so eager to get well that he keeps watching his tongue, feeling his pulse, and getting his weight. Peace does not come to one who is watching continually for the results of his work, or who is wondering what people are saying about it, or who is envious and jealous of other persons working in the same field, or who is touchy about "honor" or recognition. Those are just the attitudes which frustrate peace and make it stay away from one's inner self.

There is a higher level of work and service and ministry, which, thank God, men like us can reach. It is attained when one swings out into a way of life which is motived and controlled by genuine sincere love and devotion, when consecration obliterates self-seeking, when in some measure, like Christ, the worker can say without reservations, "Not my will but thine be done."

CHAPTER II
THE GREAT ENERGIES THAT WORK

I
TRYING THE BETTER WAY

A very fresh and unusual type of book has recently appeared under the title, *"ByAnUnknownDisciple*."It tells in a simple, direct, impressive way, after the manner of the Gospels, the story of Christ's life and works and message. It professes to be written by one who was an intimate disciple, and who was therefore an eye-witness of everything told in the book. It is a vivid narrative and leaves the reader deeply moved, because it brings him closer than most interpretations do into actual presence of and companionship with the great Galilean. The first chapter is a re-interpretation of the scene on the eastern shore of Gennesaret, where Jesus casts the demons out of the maniac of Geresa. A man on the shore of the lake told Jesus, when he landed there with his disciples in the early morning, that it was not safe for any one to go up the rugged hillside, because there were madmen hidden there among the tombs: "people possessed by demons, who tear their flesh, and who can be heard screaming day and night."

"How do you know they are possessed by demons?" asked Jesus.

"What else could it be?" said the man. "There are none that can master them. They are too fierce to be tamed."

"Has any man tried to tame them?" asked Jesus.

"Yes, Rabbi, they have been bound with chains and fetters. There was one that I saw. He plucked the fetters from him as a child might break a chain of field flowers. Then he ran foaming into the wilderness, and no man dare pass by that way now...."

"Have men tried only this way to tame him?" Jesus asked.

"What other way is there, Rabbi?" asked the man.

"There is God's way," said Jesus. "Come, let us try it."

As Jesus spoke, "His gaze went from man to man," the writer continues, "and then his eyes fell upon me. It was as if a power passed from him to me, and immediately something inside me answered, 'Lead, and I follow.'" The narrative proceeds to describe the encounter with the demoniac man whose name was "Legion." "He ran toward us, shrieking and bounding in the air. He had two sharp stones in his hand, and as he leaped he cut his flesh with them and the blood ran down his naked limbs. The men behind us scattered and fled down the hillside; but Jesus stood still and waited." The effect of the calm, undisturbed, unfrightened presence of Jesus was astonishing. It was as though a new force suddenly came into operation. The jagged stones were thrown from his hands, for he recognized at once in Jesus a friendly presence and a helper with an understanding heart. His fear and terror left the demoniac man and he became quiet, composed and like a normal person. Meantime some of the men who ran away in fear, when the madman appeared, frightened a herd of swine feeding near by, and in their uncontrolled terror they rushed wildly toward the headland of the lake and pitched over the top into the water where they were drowned. "Fear is a foul spirit," said Jesus, and it seemed plain and obvious that the ungoverned fear which played such havoc with the man had taken possession also of the misguided swine. It was the same "demon," fear. A little later in the day when the companions of Jesus found him they saw the man who had called himself "Legion" sitting at Jesus' feet, clothed and in his right mind—a quieted and restored person.

We now know that this disease, called "possession," which appears so often in the New Testament accounts, is a very common present-day trouble. The name and description given to it in the Bible make it often seem remote and unfamiliar to us, but it is, in fact, as prevalent in the world to-day as it was in the first century. It is an extreme form of hysteria, a disorganization of normal functions, often causing delusions, loss of memory, the performance of automatic actions, and sometimes resulting in double, or multiple, personality, a condition in which a foreign self seems to usurp the control of the body and make it do many strange and unwilled things. This disease is known in very many cases to be produced by frights, fear, or terror, sometimes fears long hidden away and more or less suppressed.

The famous cases of Doris Fischer and Miss Beauchamp were both of this type. They were only extreme instances of a fairly common form of mental trouble, generally due to fears, and capable of being cured by wise, skillful understanding and loving care, applied by one who shows confidence and human interest and who knows how to use the powerful influence of *suggestion.* Dr. Morton Prince, who has reported these two cases, has achieved cures and restorations that read like miracles, and his narratives tell of minds, "jangling, harsh, and out of tune," broken into dissociated selves, which have been unified, organized, harmonized and restored to normal life. Few restorations are more wonderful than that effected upon a Philadelphia girl under the direction of Dr. Lightner Witmer. The girl was hopelessly incorrigible, stubborn, sullen, suspicious, and stupid. She screamed, kicked, and bit when she was opposed, and she utterly refused to obey anybody. So unnatural and dehumanized was she that she was generally called "Diabolical Mary." She was examined by Dr. Witmer, underwent some simple surgical operations to remove her obvious physical handicaps, and then was put under the loving, tender care of a wise, attractive, and understanding woman. The girl responded to the treatment at once and soon became profoundly changed, and the process went on until the girl became a wholly transformed and re-made person.

The so-called shell-shock cases which have bulked so large in the story of the wastage of men in all armies during the World War, turn out to be cases of mental disorganization, occasioned for the most part by immense emotional upheaval, especially through suppressed fear. The man affected with the trouble has seemed to master his emotion. He has not winced or shown the slightest fear in the face of danger; but the pent-up emotion, the suppressed fear and terror, insidiously throw the entire nervous mechanism out of gear. The successful treatment of such cases is, again, like that for hysteria, one that brings confidence, calm, liberation of all strain and anxiety. The poor victim needs a patient, wise, skillful, psychologically trained physician, who has an understanding mind, a friendly, interested, intimate way, a spirit of love, and who can arouse expectation of recovery and can suggest thoughts of health and the right emotional reactions. This method of cure has often been tried with striking effect upon the so-called criminal classes. Prisoners almost always respond constructively to the personal manifestation of confidence, sympathy, and love. Elizabeth Fry proved this principle in an astonishing way with the almost brutalized prisoners in Newgate. Thomas Shillitoe's visit to the German prisoners at Spandau, who were believed to be beyond all human appeals, though not so well known and famous, is no less impressive and no less convincing.

There was perhaps never a time in the history of the world when an application of this principle and method—God's way—was so needed in the social sphere of life. Whole countries have the symptoms which appear in these nervous diseases. It is not merely an individual case here and there; it takes on a corporate, a mass, form. The nerves are overstrained, the emotional stress has been more than could be borne, suppressed fears have produced disorganization. There are signs of social "dissociation." The remedy in such cases is not an application of compelling force, not a resort to chains and fetters, not a screwing on of the "lid," not a method of starving out the victims. It is rather an application of the principle which has always worked in individual cases of "dissociation" or "possession" or "suppressed fear"—the principle of sympathy, love and suggestion—what Jesus, in the book mentioned above, calls "God's way." The "dissociation" of labor and employers in the social group, with its hysterical signs of strikes and lockouts, upheaval and threats, needs just now a very wise physician. Force, restraint, compulsion, fastening down the "lid," imprisonment of leaders, drastic laws against propaganda, will not cure the disease, any more than chains cured the poor sufferer on the shores of Gennesaret. The situation must first of all be *understood*. The inner attitude behind the acts and deeds must be taken into account. The social mental state must be diagnosed. The remedy, to be a remedy, must remove the causes which produce the dissociation. It can be accomplished only by one who has an understanding heart, a good will, an unselfish purpose, and a comprehending, i.e., a unifying, *suggestion* of coöperation.

This *way* is no less urgent for the solution of the most acute international situations. It has been assumed too long and too often that these situations can be best handled by unlimited methods of restraint, coercion, and reduction to helplessness. Some of the countries of Europe have been plainly suffering from neurasthenia, dissociation, and the kindred forms of emotional, fear-caused diseases. Starvation always makes for types of hysteria. It will not do now to apply, with cold, precise logic, the old vindictive principle that when the sinner has been made to suffer enough to "cover" the enormity of his sin he can then be restored to respectable society. It is not vindication of justice which most concerns the world now; it is a return of health, a restoration of normal functions, a reconstruction of the social body. That task calls for the application of the deeper, truer principles of life. It calls for a knowing heart, an understanding method, a healing plan, a sympathetic guide who can obliterate the fear-attitude and *suggest* confidence and unity and trustful human relationships. Those great words, used in the Epistle of London Yearly Meeting of Friends in 1917, need to be revived and put to an experimental venture: "*Love knows no frontiers.*" There is no limit to its healing force, there are no conditions it does not meet, there is no terminus to its constructive operations.

II
HE CAME TO HIMSELF

Was there ever such a short-story character sketch as this one of the prodigal son! No realism of details, no elaboration of his sins, and yet the immortal picture is burned forever into our imagination. The *débâcle* of his life is as clear and vivid as words can portray the ruin. Yet the phrase which arrests us most as we read the compact narrative of his undoing is not the one which tells about "riotous living," or the reckless squandering of his patrimony, or his hunger for swine husks, or his unshod feet and the loss of his tunic; it is rather the one which says that when he was at the bottom of his fortune "he came to himself."

He had not been himself then, before. He was not finding himself in the life of riotous indulgence. That did not turn out after all to be the life for which he was meant. He missed himself more than he missed his lost shoes and tunic. That raises a nice question which is worth an answer: When is a person his real self? When can he properly say, "At last I have found myself; I am what I want to be?" Robert Louis Stevenson has given us in Dr. Jekyll and Mr. Hyde a fine parable of the actual double self in us all, a higher and a lower self under our one hat. But I ask, which is the real me? Is it Jekyll or is it Hyde? Is it the best that we can be or is it this worse thing which we just now are?

Most answers to the question would be, I think, that the real self is that ideal self of which in moments of rare visibility we sometimes catch glimpses.

"All I could never be,
All, men ignored in me,
This, I was worth to God, whose wheel the pitcher shaped."

"Dig deep enough into any man," St. Augustine said, "and you will find something divine." We supposed he believed in total depravity, and he does in theory believe in it; but when it is a matter of actual experience, he announces this deep fact which fits perfectly with his other great utterance: "Thou, O God, hast made us for thyself, and we are restless (dissatisfied) until we find ourselves in thee."

Too long we have assumed that Adam, the failure, is the type of our lives, that he is the normal man, that to err is human, and that one touch, that is, blight, of nature makes all men kin. What Christ has revealed to us is the fact that we always have higher and diviner possibilities in us. He, the overcomer, and not Adam, is the true type, the normal person, giving us at last the pattern of life which is life indeed.

Which is the real self, then? Surely this higher possible self, this one which we discover in our best moments. The Greeks always held that sin was "missing the mark"—that is what the Greek word for sin means—failure to arrive at, to reach, the real end toward which life aims. Sin is defeat. It is loss of the trail. It is undoing. The sinner has not found himself, he has not come to himself. He has missed the real me. He cannot say, "I am."

If that is a fact, and if the life of spiritual health and attainment is the normal life, we surely ought to do more than is done to help young people to realize it and to assist them to find themselves. We are much more concerned to manufacture things than we are to make persons. We do one very well and we do the other very badly. Kipling's "The Ship that Found Itself" is a fine account of the care bestowed upon every rivet and screw, every valve and piston. He pictures the ship in the stress and strain of a great storm and each part of the ship from keel to funnel describes what it has to bear and to do in the emergency and how it has been prepared in advance for just this crisis. Nansen was asked how he felt when he found that the *Fram* was caught in the awful jam of the Arctic ice-floe. "I felt perfectly calm," he said. "I knew she could stand it. I had watched every stick of timber and every piece of steel that went into her hull. The result was that I could go to sleep and let the ice do its worst." With even more care we build the airplane. There must be no chance for capricious action. The propeller blades must be made of perfect wood. There must be no defect in any piece of the structure. The gasoline must be tested by all the methods of refinement. The oil must be absolutely pure, free of every suspicion of grit.

But when we turn from ships and airplanes to the provisions for training young persons we are in a different world. The element of chance now bulks very large. We let the youth have pretty free opportunity to begin his malformation before we begin seriously to construct him on right lines. We fail to note what an enormous fact "disposition" is, and we take little pains to form it early and to form it in the best way. We are far too apt to assume that all the fundamentals come by the road of heredity. We overwork this theory as much as earlier theologians overworked their dogma of original sin from poor old Adam.

The fact is that temperament and disposition and the traits of character which most definitely settle destiny are at least as much formed in those early critical years of infancy as they are acquired by the strains of heredity. Education, which is more essential to the greatness of any country than even its manufactures, is one of the most neglected branches of life. We take it as we find it—and lay its failures to Providence as we do deaths from typhoid. It must not always be so. We must be as greatly concerned to form virile character in our boys and girls and to develop in them the capacity for moral and spiritual leadership in this crisis as we are concerned over our coal supply or our industries. There are ways of assisting the higher self to control and dominate the life, ways by which the ideal person can become the real person. Why not consider seriously how to do that?

He that overcomes, the prophet of Patmos says, receives a white stone with a new name written on it, which no man knoweth save he that hath it. It is a symbolism which may mean many things. It seems at least to mean that he who subdues his lower self, holds out in the strain of life, and lives by the highest that he knows, will as a consequence receive a distinct individuality, a clearly defined self, instead of being blurred in with the great level mass—a self with a name of its own. And that self will not be the old familiar self that everybody knows by traits of past achievement and by the old tendencies of habit. It will be the self which only God and the person himself in his deepest and most intimate moments knew was possible—and here at last it is found to be the real self. The man can say, "I am." He has come to himself.

We ask, at the end, whether it may not be that the world will soon come to itself and discover the way back to some of its missed ideals. Here on a large scale we have the story of a desperate hunger, squandered wealth, lost shoes, lost tunics, and even more precious things gone—a world that has missed its way and is floundering about without sufficient vision or adequate leadership. If it could only come to itself, discover what its true mission is and where its real sources of power and its line of progress lie, it would still find that God and man together can rebuild what man by his blunders has destroyed.

III
SOME NEW REASONS FOR "LOVING ENEMIES"

Nobody ever amounts to anything who lives without conflict with obstacles. It seems to be a law of the universe that nothing really good can be got or held by soft, easy means.

The Persians were so impressed with this stern condition of life that they interpreted the universe as the scene of endless warfare between hostile powers of the invisible world. Ormuzd, the god of light, and Ahriman, the god of darkness, were believed to be engaged in a continual Armageddon. There could be no truce in the strife until one or the other should win the victory by the annihilation of his opponent. This Persian dualism has touched all systems of thought and has left its influence upon all the religions of the world. The reasons why it has appealed so powerfully to men of all generations are, of course, that there is so much conflict involved in life and that no achievement of goodness is ever made without a hard battle for it against opposing forces. But if all this opposition and struggle is due to an "enemy," we certainly ought to love this "enemy," because it turns out to be the greatest possible blessing to us that we are forced to struggle with difficulties and to wrestle for what we get.

"Count it all joy," said the Apostle James in substance, writing to his friends of the Dispersion, "when you fall into manifold testings, or trials, knowing that the proving of your faith worketh steadfastness, and let steadfastness have its perfect work, that ye may be perfect and entire, lacking in nothing." St. Paul thought once that his "thorn in the flesh" was conferred upon him by Satan and was the malicious messenger of an enemy; but in the slow process of experience he came to see that the painful "thorn" exercised a real ministry in his life, that through his suffering and hardship he got a higher meaning of God's grace; and he discovered that divine power was thus made perfect through his weakness, so that he learned to love the "enemy" that buffeted him.

The Psalmist who wrote our best loved psalm, the twenty-third, thought at first that God was his Shepherd because he led him in green pastures and beside still waters where there was no struggle and no enemy to fear. But he learned at length that in the dark valleys of the shadow and on the rough jagged hillsides God was no less a good Shepherd than on the level plains and in the lush grass; and he found at last that even "in the presence of enemies" he could be fed with good things and have his table spread. The overflowing cup and the anointed head were not discovered on the lower levels of ease and comfort; they came out of the harder experiences when "enemies" of his peace were busy supplying obstacles and perplexities for him to overcome.

It is no accident that the book of Revelation puts so much stress upon "overcoming." The world seemed to the prophet on the volcanic island of Patmos essentially a place of strife and conflict—an Armageddon of opposing forces. There are no beatitudes in this book promised to any except "overcomers."

> "Not to one church alone, but seven
> The voice prophetic spake from heaven;
> And unto each the promise came,
> Diversified, but still the same;
> For him that overcometh are
> The new name written on the stone,
> The raiment white, the crown, the throne,
> And I will give him the Morning Star!"

But the conflict that ends in such results can not be called misfortune, any more than Hercules' labors through which the legendary hero won his immortality can be pronounced a misfortune for him. Once more, then, the saint who has overcome discovers, at least in retrospect, that there is good ground for loving his "enemies"!

The farmer, in his unceasing struggle with weeds, with parasites, with pests visible and invisible, with blight and rot and uncongenial weather, sometimes feels tempted to blaspheme against the hard conditions under which he labors and to assume that an "enemy" has cursed the ground which he tills and loaded the dice of nature against him. The best cure for his "mood" is to visit the land of the bread-fruit tree, where nature does everything and man does nothing but eat what is gratuitously given him, and to see there the kind of men you get under those kindly skies. The virile fiber of muscle, the strong manly frame, the keen active mind that meets each new "pest" with a successful invention, the spirit of conquest and courage that are revealed in the farmer at his best are no accident. They are the by-product of his battle with conditions, which if they seem to come from an "enemy," must come from one that ought to be loved for what he accomplishes.

These critics of ours who harshly review the books we write, the addresses we give, the schemes of reform for which we work so strenuously —do they do nothing for us? On the contrary, they force us to go deeper, to write with more care, to reconsider our hasty generalizations, to recast our pet schemes, to revise our crude endeavors. They may speak as "enemies," and they may show a stern and hostile face; but we do well to love them, for they enable us to find our better self and our deeper powers. The hand may be the horny hand of Esau, but the voice is the kindly voice of Jacob.

All sorts of things "work" for us, then, as St. Paul declared. Not only does love "work," and faith and grace; but tribulation "works," and affliction, and the seemingly hostile forces which block and buffet and hamper us. Everything that drives us deeper, that draws us closer to the great resources of life, that puts vigor into our frame and character into our souls, is in the last resort a blessing to us, even though it seems on superficial examination to be the work of an "enemy," and we shall be wise if we learn to love the "enemies" that give us the chance to overcome and to attain our true destiny. Perhaps the dualism of the universe is not quite as sharp as the old Persians thought. Perhaps, too, the love of God reaches further under than we sometimes suppose. Perhaps in fact all things "work together for good," and even the enemy forces are helping to achieve the ultimate good that shall be revealed "when God hath made the pile complete."

CHAPTER III
THE POWER THAT WORKETH IN US

I
WHERE THE BEYOND BREAKS THROUGH

If we sprinkle iron filings over a sheet of paper and move a magnet beneath the paper, the filings become active and combine and recombine in a great variety of groupings and regroupings. A beholder who knows nothing of the magnet underneath gazes upon the whole affair with a sense of awe and mystery, though he feels all the time that there must be some explanation of the action and that some hidden power behind is operating as the cause of the groupings and regroupings of the iron particles. Something certainly that we do not see is revealing its presence and its power.

Our everyday experience is full of another series of activities even more mysterious than these movements of the iron. Whenever we open our eyes we see objects and colors confronting us and located in spaces far and near. What brings the object to us? What operates to produce the contact? How does the far-away thing hit our organ of vision? This was to the ancient philosopher a most difficult problem, a real mystery. He made many guesses at a solution, but no guess which he could make satisfied his judgment. Our answer is that an invisible and intangible substance which we call ether—luminiferous ether—fills all space, even the space occupied by visible objects, and that this ether which is capable of amazing vibrations, billions of them a second, is set vibrating at different velocities by different objects. These vibrations bombard the minute rods and cones of the retina at the back of the eye and, presto, we see now one color and now another, now one object and now another. This ether would forever have remained unknown to us had not this marvelous structure of the retina given it a chance to break through and reveal itself. In many other ways, too, this ether breaks through into revelation. It is responsible apparently for all the immensely varied phenomena of electricity, probably, too, of cohesion and gravitation. Here, again, the revelations remained inadequate and without clear interpretation until we succeeded in constructing proper instruments and devices for it to break through into active operation. The dynamo and the other electrical mechanisms which we have invented do not make or create electricity. They merely let it come through, showing itself now as light, now as heat, now again as motive power. But always it was there before, unnoted, merely potential, and yet a vast surrounding ocean of energy there behind, ready to break into active operation when the medium was at hand for it.

Life is another one of those strange mysteries that cannot be explained until we realize that something more than we see is breaking through matter and revealing itself. The living thing is letting through some greater power than itself, something beyond and behind, which is needed to account for what we see moving and acting with invention and purpose. Matter of itself is no explanation of life. The same elemental stuff is very different until it becomes the instrument of something not itself which organizes it, pushes it upward and onward, and reveals itself through it. Something has at length come into view which is more than force and mechanism. Here is intelligent purpose and forward-looking activity and something capable of variation, novelty, and surprise. And when living substance has reached a certain stage of organization, something higher still begins to break through—consciousness appears, and on its higher levels consciousness begins to reveal truth and moral goodness. It is useless to try to explain consciousness—especially truth-bearing consciousness—as a function of the brain, for it cannot be done. That way of explanation no more explains mind than the Ptolemaic theory explains the movements of the heavenly bodies. Once more, something breaks through and reveals itself, as surely as light breaks through a prism and reveals itself in the band of spectral colors. This consciousness of ours, as I have said, is not merely awareness, not only intelligent response; it lays hold of and apprehends, i.e., reveals, truth and goodness. What I think, when I really think, is not just my private "opinion," or "guess," or "seeming"; it turns out to have something universal and absolute about it. My multiplication-table is everybody's multiplication-table. It is true for me and for beyond me. And what is true of my mathematics is also true of other features of my thinking. When I properly organize my experience through rightly formed concepts, I express aspects that are real and true for everybody—I attain to something which can be called truth. The same way in the field of conduct: I can discover not only what is subjectively right, but I can go farther and embody principles which are right not only for me but for every good man. Something more than a petty, tiny, private consciousness is expressing itself through my personality. I am the organ of something more than myself.

Perhaps more wonderful still is the way in which beauty breaks through. It breaks through not only at a few highly organized points, it breaks through almost everywhere. Even the minutest things reveal it as well as do the sublimest things, like the stars. Whatever one sees through the microscope, a bit of mould for example, is charged with beauty. Everything from a dewdrop to Mount Shasta is the bearer of beauty. And yet beauty has no function, no utility. Its value is intrinsic, not extrinsic. It is its own excuse for being. It greases no wheels, it bakes no puddings. It is a gift of sheer grace, a gratuitous largess. It must imply behind things a Spirit that enjoys beauty for its own sake and that floods the world everywhere with it. Wherever it can break through it does break through, and our joy in it shows that we are in some sense kindred to the giver and revealer of it.

Something higher and greater still breaks through and reveals a deeper Reality than any that we see and touch. Love comes through—not everywhere like beauty, but only where rare organization has prepared an organ for it. Some aspects of love appear very widely, are, at least, as universal as truth and moral goodness. But love in its full glory, love in its height of unselfishness and with its passion of self-giving is a rare manifestation. One person—the Galilean—has been a perfect revealing organ of it. In his life it broke through with the same perfect naturalness as the beam of light breaks through the prism of waterdrops and reveals the rainbow. Love that understands, sympathizes, endures, inspires, recreates, and transforms, broke through and revealed itself so impressively that those who see it and feel it are convinced that here at last the real nature of God has come through to us and stands revealed. And St. Paul, who was absolutely convinced of this, went still further. He held, with a faith buttressed in experience, that this same Christ, who had made this demonstration of love, became after his resurrection an invisible presence, a life-giving Spirit who could work and act as a resident power within receptive, responsive, human spirits, and could transform them into a likeness to himself and continue his revelation of love wherever he should find such organs of revelation. If that, or something like it, is true it is a very great truth. It was this that good old William Dell meant when he said:

"The believer is the only book in which God himself writes his New Testament."

II
CONQUERING BY AN INNER FORCE

There are few texts that have been more dynamic in the history of spiritual religion than the one which forms the keynote of the message of the little book of Habakkuk: "The righteous man lives by faith" (2:4). It became the central feature of St. Paul's message. It was the epoch-making discovery in Luther's experience, and it has always been the guiding principle of Protestant Christianity.

The profound significance of the words is often missed because the text is so easily turned into a phrase that is supposed just of itself to work a kind of magic spell, and secondly because the meaning of "faith" is so frequently misinterpreted. When we go back to the original experience out of which the famous text was born we can get fresh light upon the heart of its meaning. The little book begins with a searching analysis of the conditions of the time. With an almost unparalleled boldness the prophet challenges God to explain why the times are so badly out of joint, why the social order is so topsy-turvy, and why injustice is allowed to run a long course unchecked. God seems unconcerned with affairs—the moral pilot appears not to be steering things.

Then comes a moment of mental relief. The prophet hits upon the conclusion, arrived at by other prophets also, that God is about to use the Chaldeans as a divine instrument to chastise the wicked element in the nation, to right the wrongs of the disordered world, and to execute judgment. But as he begins to reflect he becomes more perplexed than ever. How can God, who is good, use such a terrible instrument for moral purposes? This people, which is assumed to be an instrument of moral judgment in a disordered world, is itself unspeakably perverse. It is fierce and wolfish. Its only god is might. It cares only for success. It catches men, like fish, in its great dragnet, and "then he sacrificeth unto his net and burneth incense unto his drag." How can such a pitiless and insolent people, dominated by pride and love of conquest, be used to work out the ends of righteousness and to act for God who is too pure even to look upon that which is evil and wrong? Here the prophet finds himself suddenly up against the ancient problem of the moral government of the universe and the deep mystery of evil in it. He cannot untangle the snarled threads of his skein. No solution of the mystery lies at hand. He decides to climb up into his "watch-tower" and wait for an answer from God. If it does not come at once, he proposes to stay until it does come—"if it tarry, wait for it; it will surely come." At length the vision comes, so clear that a man running can read it. It is just this famous discovery of the great text that a man cannot hope to get the world-difficulties all straightened out to suit him, he cannot in some easy superficial way justify the ways of God in the course of history; but, at least, he can live unswervingly and victoriously by his own soul's insight, the insight of faith that God can be trusted to do the right thing for the universe which he is steering. It is beautifully expressed in a well-known stanza of Whittier's:

"I know not where His islands lift
Their fronded palms in air;
I only know I cannot drift
Beyond His love and care."

Many things remain unexplained. The mysteries are not all dissipated. But I see enough light to enable me to hold a steady course onward, and I have an inner confidence in God which nothing in the outward world can shatter. This is the message from Habakkuk's watch-tower: There is a faith which goes so far into the heart of things that a man can live by it and stand all the water-spouts which break upon him.

Josiah Royce once defined faith as an insight of the soul by which one can stand everything that can happen to him, and that is what this text means. You arrive at such a personal assurance of God's character that you can face any event and not be swept off your feet. If this is so, it means that the most important achievement in a man's career is the attainment of just this inner vision, the acquisition of an interior spiritual confidence which itself is the victory.

William James used often to close his lecture courses at Harvard with what he called a "Faith-ladder." Round after round it went up from a mere possibility of hope to an inner conviction strong enough to dominate action.

He would begin with some human faith which outstrips evidence and he would say of it: It is at least not absurd, not self-contradictory, and, therefore, it might be true under certain conditions, in some kind of a world which we can conceive. It may be true even in this world and under existing conditions. It is fit to be true; it ought to be true. The soul in its moment of clearest insight feels that it must be true. It shall be true, then, at least for me, for I propose to act upon it, to live by it, to stake my existence on it.

This watch-tower of Habakkuk is a similar faith-ladder. He sees no way to explain why the good suffer, or to account for the catastrophes of history, but at least he has found a faith in God which holds him like adamant: "Although the fig-tree shall not blossom, neither shall fruit be in the vines; the labor of the olive shall fail, and the fields shall yield no meat; the flock shall be cut off from the fold and there shall be no herd in the stalls: Yet I will rejoice in the Lord, I will joy in the God of my salvation.... He will make me to walk upon mine high places." Faith like that is always contagious. The unshaken soul kindles another soul who believes in his belief, and the torch goes from this man on his watch-tower to St. Paul, and from him on to the great reformer, and then to an unnamed multitude, who through their soul's insight can stand everything that may happen!

III
LIVING IN THE PRESENCE OF THE ETERNAL

Some time ago I received a letter from a young minister who was about to settle for religious work in a large manufacturing town. He and I were strangers to each other in the flesh but friends through correspondence, and because we were kindred spirits he wrote to me to say: "I have before me the great work of living in the eternal God and in a humanity toiling in factories and shops. Oh, if I could only make the presence of the Eternal real to myself and to my people!" Another minister, laboring in a large suburb of New York City, also a stranger to me except through correspondence, wrote to say that he was glad for every voice which holds up before men the reality of the invisible Church and the idea of the universal priesthood of believers. These letters coming within a week—and they are samples of many similar ones—are signs of the times, and show clearly that thoughtful men all about us are done with the husk of religion and are devoting themselves to the heart of the matter. There is a deep movement under way which touches all denominations and is steadily preparing in our busy, hurrying, materialistic America a true seed of the vital, spiritual religion that will later bear rich blossoms and ripe harvest.

I want for the moment to return to the central desire of the young minister, in the hope that it may inspire some of us, especially some of our young ministers who are facing their new spiritual tasks: "I have before me the great work of living in the eternal God and in a humanity toiling in factories and shops. Oh, if I could only make the presence of the Eternal real to myself and to them!"

It is perhaps a new idea to some that living in the eternal God is "work." We are so accustomed to the idea that all that is required of us is a passive mind and a waiting spirit that we have never quite realized this truth: No person can live in the eternal God unless he is ready for the most intense activity and for the most strenuous life. Gladstone, in his old age, surprised his readers with his impressive phrase, "the work of worship." The fact is, no man ever yet found his way into the permanent enjoyment of God along paths of least resistance or by any lazy methods. How many of us have been humiliated to discover, in the silence or in the service, that nothing spiritual was happening within us. Our mind, unbent and passive enough, was like a stagnant pool, or, if not stagnant, was darting its feelers out and following in lazy fashion any line of suggestion which pulled it. Instead of finding ourselves "living in the eternal God" and in the high enjoyment of him, we catch ourselves wondering what the next strike will be, or thinking about the mean and shabby way some one spoke to us an hour ago! There is no use blaming a mind because it wanders—everybody's mind wanders—but the real achievement is to make it wander in a region which ministers to our spiritual life; and that can be done only by getting supremely interested in the things of the Spirit. That is where the "work" lies; that is where the effort comes in. Attention is always determined by the fundamental interest. What we love supremely we attend to. It gets us, it holds us. One of the colloquial phrases for being in love with a person is "paying attention to" the person. It is a true phrase and goes straight to reality. If we are to discover and enjoy the eternal Presence we must become passionately earnest in spirit and glowing with love for the Highest.

My friend brings two important things together: He proposes to undertake the work of living in the eternal God and in toiling humanity. The two things go together and cannot be safely separated. It is in the actual sharing of life through love and sympathy and sacrifice, in going out of self to feel the problems and difficulties and sufferings of others, that we find and form a life rich in higher interests and centered on matters of eternal value. A man who has traveled through the deeps of life with a fellow man comes to his hour of worship with a mind focused on the Eternal and with a spirit girded for the inward wrestling, without which blessings of the greater sort do not come. And every time such a man finds himself truly at home in the eternal God and fed from within, he can go out, with the strength of ten, to the tasks of toiling humanity. This is one of those spiritual circles which work both ways: He that dwells in God loves, and he that loves finds God, St. John tells us.

It is fine to see a strong man, trained in all his faculties, going to his work with the quiet prayer: "Oh, that I may make the presence of the Eternal real to myself and to my people." It is a good prayer for all of us.

CHAPTER IV
THE WAY OF VISION

I
DAYS OF GREATER VISIBILITY

From the porch of my little summer cottage in Maine I can see, across the beautiful stretch of lake in the foreground, the far-distant Kennebago Mountains in their veil of purple. But we see them only when all the conditions of sky and air are absolutely right. Most of the time they are wrapped in clouds or are lost in a dim haze. Our visitors admire the lake, are charmed with the islands, the picturesque shore and the surrounding hills, but they do not suspect the existence of this added glory beyond the hills. We often tell them of the mountains "just over there," which come out into full view when the sky clears all the way to the horizon and the wind blows fine from the northwest. They make a casual remark about the sufficiency of what is already in sight, and go their way in satisfied ignorance of the "beyond."

Next day, perhaps—Oh wonder! The morning dawns with all the conditions favorable for our distant view. The air is altogether right for far visibility. The clouds are swept clean from the western rim, the blue is utterly transparent—and there are the mountains! We wish our skeptical visitors could be with us now. We guess that they would not easily talk of the sufficiency of the near beauty, if they could once see the overtopping glory of these mountains now fully unveiled and revealed. Something like that, I feel sure, is true of God and of other great spiritual realities which are linked with his being. Most of the time we get on with the things that are near at hand; the things we see and handle and are sure of. The world is full of utility and we do well to appreciate what is there waiting to be used. There is always something satisfying about beauty, and nature is very rich and lavish with it. Friendship and love are heavenly gifts, and when these are added to the other good things which the world gives us, it would seem, and it does seem, to many that we ought to be satisfied and not be homesick for the glory which lies beyond the horizon-line of the senses. I cannot help it; my soul will not stay satisfied with this near-at-hand supply. A discontent sweeps over me, an uncontrollable *Heimweh*—homesickness of soul—surges up within me and I should be compelled to call the whole scheme miserable failure, if the near, visible skyline were the real boundary of all that is.

Sometimes—Oh joy! When the inward weather is just right; when selfish impulse has been hushed; when the clouds and shadows, which sin makes, are swept away and genuine love makes the whole inner atmosphere pure and free from haze, then I know that I find a beyond which before was nowhere in sight and might easily not have been suspected. I cannot decide whether this extended range of sight is due to alterations in myself, or whether it is due to some sudden increase of spiritual visibility in the great reality itself. I only know the fact. Before, I was occupied with things; now, I commune with God and am as sure of him as I am of the mountains beyond my lake, which my skeptical visitor has not yet seen.

There can be no adequate world here for us without at least a faith in the reality beyond the line of what we see with our common eyes. We have times when we cannot live by bread alone, or by our increase of stocks; when we lose our interest in cosmic forces and need something more than the slow justice which history weighs out on its great judgment days. We want to feel a real heart beating somewhere through things; we want to discover through the maze a loving will working out a purpose; we want to know that our costly loyalties, our high endeavors, and our sacrifices which make the quivering flesh palpitate with pain, really matter to Someone and fill up what is behind of his great suffering for love's sake. We can not get on here with substitutes; we must have the reality itself. Religion is an awful farce if it is only a play-scheme, a cinematograph-show, which makes one believe he is seeing reality when he is, in fact, being fooled with a picture. We must at all costs insist on the real things. It is God we want and not another, the real Face and not a picture.

"We needs must love the highest when we see it;
Not Lancelot nor another."

He is surely there to be seen, like my mountain. Days may pass when we only hope and long and guess. Then the weather comes right, the veil thins away and we see! It is, however, not a rare privilege reserved for a tiny few. It is not a grudged miracle, granted only to saints who have killed out all self. It belongs to the very nature of the soul to see God. It is what makes life really life. It is as normal a function as breathing or digestion. Only one must, of all things, intend to do it!

II
THE PROPHET AND HIS TRAGEDIES

There will always be in the world a vast number of persons who take the most comfortable form of religion which their generation affords. They are not path-breakers; they have nothing in their nature which pushes them into the fields of discovery—they are satisfied with the religion which has come down to them from the past. They accept what others have won and tested, and are thankful that they are saved the struggle and the fire which are involved in first-hand experience and in fresh discovery.

The prophet, on the contrary, in whatever age he comes, can never take this easy course. He cannot rest contented with the forms of religion which are accepted by others. He cannot enjoy the comforts of the calm and settled faith which those around him inherit and adopt. His soul forever hears the divine call to leave the old mountain and go forward, to conquer new fields, to fight new battles, to restate his faith in words that are fresh and vital, in terms of the deepest life of his time. We used to think—many people still think—that a prophet is a foreteller of future events, a kind of magical and miraculous person who speaks as an oracle and who announces, without knowing how or why, far-off, coming occurrences that are communicated to him. To think thus is to miss the deeper truth of the prophet's mission. He is primarily a religious patriot, a statesman with a moral and spiritual policy for the nation. He is a person who sees what is involved in the eternal nature of things and therefore what the outcome of a course of life is bound to be. He possesses an unerring eye for curves of righteousness or unrighteousness, as the great artist has for lines of beauty and harmony, or as the great mathematician has for the completing lines of a curve, involved in any given arc of it. He is different from others, not in the fact that he has ecstasies and lives in the realm of miracles, but rather that he has a clearer conviction of God than most men have. He has found him as the center of all reality. He reads and interprets all history in the light of the indubitable fact of God, and he estimates life and deeds in terms of moral and spiritual laws, which are as inflexible as the laws of chemical atoms or of electrical forces. He looks for no capricious results. He sees that this is a universe of moral and spiritual order.

If he is an Amos, he will refuse to fall in line with the easy worshipers of his age, who are satisfied with the old-time religion of "burnt offerings" and "meat offerings" and "peace offerings of fat beasts." His soul will cry out for a religion which makes a new moral and spiritual man, "makes righteousness run down as a mighty stream," and sets the worshiper into new social relations with his fellows. If he is an Isaiah, he will refuse "to tramp the temple" with the mass of easy worshipers; he will have his own vision of "the Lord high and lifted up," with his glory filling not only the temple but the whole earth, and he will dedicate himself to the task of preparing a holy people and a holy city for this God who has been revealed to him as a thrice-holy God. If he is a Jeremiah, he will not accept the view that the traditional religion of Jerusalem is adequate for the crisis of the times. He will insist that true religion must be inwardly experienced; that the law of God must be written in the heart, and that the life of a man must be the living fruit of his faith. He will cry out against the idea that the moral wounds and spiritual sores of the daughter of Jerusalem can be healed with easy salves and cheap panaceas.

The supreme example of this refusal to go along the easy line of contemporary religion is that of One who was more than a prophet. His people prided themselves on being the chosen people of the Lord. The scribal leaders had succeeded in drawing up a complete and perfect catalogue of religious performances. They supplied minute directions for one's religious duty in every detail, real or imaginary, of daily life, and the world has never seen a more elaborate form of religion than this of the Pharisees. But Christ refused to follow the path of custom; he could not and he would not do the things which the scribes prescribed. He broke a new path for the soul, and called men away from legalism and the dead routine of "performances" to a life of individual faith and service, which involves suffering and self-sacrifice, but which brings the soul into personal relation with the living God.

St. Paul, a Pharisee of the Pharisees, a rabbinical scholar of the first rank, a man rising stage by stage to fame along the path marked out by the traditions of his people, came back from his eventful journey to Damascus to take up the work of a path-breaker and to set himself like a flint against the old-time religion in which he was born and reared. Luther, a devout monk, an ambassador to the papal court, a professor of scholastic theology, discovered that he could not find peace to his soul along the path of the prevailing traditional religion, and he swung, with all the fervor of his powerful nature, into a fresh track which has blessed all ages since. These are some of the supreme leaders, but every age has had its quota of minor prophets, who have heard the call to leave the old mountain and go forward and who have fearlessly entered the perilous and untried path of fresh vision. As we look back and see them in the perspective of their successful mission to the race, we thank God for their bravery and their valiant service, but we are apt to forget the tragedies of their lives.

Nobody can enter a fresh path, or bring a new vision of the meaning of life, or reinterpret old truths—in short, nobody can be a prophet—without arousing the suspicion and, sooner or later, the bitter hatred of those who are the keepers and guardians of the existing forms and traditions, and the path-breaker must expect to see his old friends misunderstand him, turn against him, and reproach him. He must endure the hard experience of being called a destroyer of the very things he is giving his life to build. Christ is, for example, hurried to the cross as a blasphemer, and each prophet, in his degree, has had to hear himself charged with being the very opposite of what he really is in heart and life. To be a prophet at all he must be a sensitive soul, and yet he must live and work in a pitiless rain of misunderstanding and attack. Still more tragic, perhaps, is the necessity which the prophet is under of doing his hard tasks without living to see the triumphant results. He is, naturally, ahead of his time—a path-breaker—and his contemporaries are always slow to discover and to realize what he is doing. Even those who love him and appreciate him only half see his true purpose, and thus he feels alone and solitary, though he may be in the thick of the throng. It is only when he is long dead and the mists have cleared away that he is called a prophet and comes to his true place. While he lived he was sure of only one Friend who completely understood him and approved of his course, and that was his invisible and heavenly Friend. But in spite of the tragedy and the pain and the hard road, the prophet, "seeing him who is invisible," prefers to all other paths, however easy and popular, the path of his vision and call.

III
A LONG DISTANCE CALL

Just when life seems peculiarly crowded with items of complexity and importance, the telephone rings a determined, significant kind of ring. This is evidently no ordinary passing-the-time-of-day affair. I interrupt my weighty concerns and take up the receiver with expectation. I say "Hello!" but there is no answer, no human recognition. The wire hums and buzzes, instruments click far away, plugs are pulled out and pushed in. Little tiny scraps of remote, inane, unintelligible conversation between unknown mortals furnish the only evidence I get that there is any human purpose going forward in this strange world inside the telephone system where I can see nothing happening.

Suddenly a voice which is evidently hunting for me breaks in: "Is this Mr. ———?" "Yes." "Hold the wire, please." I am led on with increasing interest and confidence. Somebody somewhere miles away in this invisible world of electrical connections is seeking for me. I forget the multitudinous problems that were besieging me when the telephone first rang, and I listen with suppressed breath and strained muscles. All I get, however, is an immense confusion. There is no coherence or order to anything that reaches me. Faint and far away in some still remoter center than at first I hear clicks and buzzes, vague unmeaning noises, and the dull thud of shifting plugs that connect the lines. Once more a kindly voice breaks in on the confusion, a voice seeking after me from some distant city: "Is this Mr. ———?" "Yes." "Wait a minute."

I do wait a minute as patiently as I can. I dimly feel that we are plunging out into yet remoter space, and that I am being connected up with the person who all the time has been seeking me. A low hum of the far-away wire is all I get to repay me for the long wait. I grow impatient. I shout "Hello!" "Is anybody there?" "Do you want me?" Not a word comes back, only endless, empty murmurs of people who have found one another and are talking so far off that the sense is lost in the mere broth of sounds. This dull world inside the telephone seems to be a mad world of noise and confusion but no substance, no real correspondence. I am on the verge of giving the whole business up and of returning to my interrupted tasks, which at least were rational.

Suddenly a voice breaks in, this time a voice I know and recognize. The person who had been seeking me all the time, across these spaces and over this network of interlaced wires, calls me by name, speaks words of insight and intelligence, and gives me a message which moves me deeply and raises the whole tone of my spirit. When finally I "hang up" and return to the things in hand, I have renewed my strength and can work with clearer head and faster pace. The pause has been like a pause in a piece of music. It has been full of significance, and it has helped toward a higher level.

Something like this telephone experience happens in another and very different sphere—a sphere where there are no wires. In the hush and silence, when the conditions are right for it, it often seems as though some one were trying to communicate with us, seeking for actual correspondence with us. We turn from the din and turmoil of busy efforts and listen for the voice. We listen intently and we hear—our own heart beating. We feel the strain of our muscles across the chest. We push back a little deeper and try again. We feel the tension of the skin over the forehead and we note that we are pulling the eyeballs up and inward for more concentrated meditation. All the muscles of the scalp are drawn and we notice them perhaps for the first time. Strange little bits of thought flit across the threshold of the mind. We catch glimpses of dim ideas knocking at the windows for admission to the inner domain where we live. Then, all of a sudden, we succeed in pushing further back. We forget our strained muscles and are unconscious of the corporeal bulk of ourselves. We get in past the flitting thoughts and the procession of ideas contending for entrance. The track seems open for the Someone who is seeking us no less certainly than we are seeking him. If we do not hear our name called, and do not hear distinctly a message in well-known words, we do at least feel that we have found a real Presence and have received fresh vital energy from the creative center of life itself, so that we come back to action, after our pause, restored, refreshed, and "charged" with new force to live by.

Some time ago a long distance call came to my telephone and I went through all the stages of waiting and of confusion and finally heard the clear voice calling me, but I could not get any answer back. I heard perfectly across the five hundred intervening miles, but my correspondent never got a single clear word from me. We found that something was wrong with our transmitter. The connection was good, the line was pervious, the seeking voice was at the other end, but I did not succeed in transmitting what ought to have been said. Here is where most of us fail in this other sphere—this inner wireless sphere—we are poor transmitters. We make the connection, we receive the gift of grace, we are flooded with the incomes of life and power and we freely take, but we do not give. We absorb and accumulate what we can, but we transmit little of all that comes to us. Our radius of out-giving influence is far too small. We need, on the one hand, to listen deeper, to get further in beyond the tensions and the noises, but on the other hand we need to be more radio-active, better transmitters of the grace of God.

CHAPTER V
THE WAY OF PERSONALITY

I
ANOTHER KIND OF HERO

A generation ago almost everybody read, at least once, Carlyle's great book on heroes. He gave us the hero as prophet, as priest, as poet, as king, and he made us realize that these heroes have been the real makers of human society. I should like to add a chapter on another kind of hero, who has, perhaps, not done much to build cities and states and church systems, but who has, almost more than anybody else, shown us the spiritual value of endurance—I mean the hero as invalid.

It is the hardest kind of heroism there is to achieve. Most of us know some man—too often it is oneself—who is a very fair Christian when he is in normal health and absorbed in interesting work, who carries a smooth forehead and easily drops into a good-natured smile, but who becomes "blue" and irritable and a storm center in the family weather as soon as the bodily apparatus is thrown out of gear. Most of us have had a taste of humiliation as we have witnessed our own defeat in the presence of some thorn in the flesh, which stubbornly pricked us, even though we prayed to have it removed and urged the doctor to hurry up and remove it.

What a hero, then, must he be, who, with a weak and broken body, a prey to pain and doomed to die daily, learns how to live in calm faith that God is good and makes his life a center of cheer and sunshine! The heroism of the battlefield and the man-of-war looks cheap and thin compared with this. We could all rally to meet some glorious moment when a trusted leader shouted to us, "Your country expects you to do your duty!" But to drag on through days and nights, through weeks and months, through recurring birthdays, with vital energy low, with sluggish appetite, with none of that ground-swell of superfluous vigor which makes healthy life so good, and still to prove that life is good and to radiate joy and triumph—that is the very flower and perfume of heroism. If we are making up a bead-roll of heroes, let us put at the top the names of those quiet friends of ours who have played the man or revealed the woman through hard periods of invalidism and have exhibited to us the fine glory of a courageous spirit.

One of the hardest and most difficult features to bear is the inability to work at one's former pace and with the old-time constructive power. The prayer of the Psalmist that his work, the contribution of his life, might be preserved is very touching: "Establish thou the work of our hands upon us, yea, the work of our hands establish thou it." What can be more tragic than the cry of Othello: "My occupation is gone!" So long as the hand keeps its cunning and the mind remains clear and creative, one can stand physical handicap and pain, but when the working power of mind or body is threatened, then the test of faith and heroism indeed arrives.

A man whose life meant much to me and whose intimacy was very precious to me made me see many years ago how wonderfully this test could be met. He was a great teacher, the head of a distinguished boys' school. He was experiencing the full measure of success, and his influence over his boys was extraordinary. He realized, as his work went on, that his hearing was becoming dull and was steadily failing. He went to New York and consulted a famous specialist. After making a careful examination the specialist said, with perfect frankness: "Your case is hopeless. Nothing can be done to check the disaster. You are hard of hearing already, but in a very short time you will have no hearing at all." Without a quaver the teacher said: "Don't you think, doctor, that I shall hear Gabriel's trumpet when it blows!" He went back to his school, learned to read lips, reorganized his life, accepted without a murmur his loss of a major sense, and finished his splendid career of work in an undefeated spirit and with a grace and joy which were envied by many persons in possession of all their powers.

All my readers will think of some "star player" in this hard game of patience and endurance, and will have watched with awe and reverence the glorious fight of some of those unrecorded heroes who won but got no valor medal. The only person who ranks higher in the scale of heroism than the hero as invalid is possibly the person who patiently, lovingly nurses and cares for some invalid through years of decline and suffering. Generally, though not always, it is a woman. Not seldom she is called upon to consecrate her life to the task, and often she gives what is much more precious than life itself. We build no monuments to daughters who unmurmuringly forego the joy of married life, who refuse the suit of love in order to be free to ease the closing years of father or mother, grown helpless; but where is there higher consecration or finer heroism? Men sometimes complain that the days of chivalry and heroism are past. On the contrary, they are more truly dawning. As Christianity ripens love grows richer and deeper, and where love appears heroism is always close at hand. Our best heroes are mothers and wives and daughters, fathers and husbands and sons.

II
THE BETTER POSSESSION

During one of the intense persecutions by which an early Roman emperor harried the Christians of the first century, some unknown writer (Harnack thinks It was a woman) wrote an extraordinary little book to hearten those who were undergoing the trial of their faith. I mean, of course, the Epistle to the Hebrews. It is marked by rare genius and by undoubted inspiration. It is full of vital messages and it contains passages of great power. Just before the most loved section of the little book—the account of the faith-heroes— the author, in a passage open to a variety of translations, refers to the fact that those to whom he is writing have suffered, and have suffered joyfully, the spoiling of their possessions, "knowing," he says, "that you have your own selves for a better possession"—you yourselves are a better possession than any of those goods which you have lost for your faith.

I wonder if the readers fully realized the truth, or if we should to-day realize it had we suffered a similar stripping. We are very slow to take account of that type of stock. We are very keen about our own assets, but we often fail to prize this supreme ownership, the possession of ourselves. There is a story, both sad and amusing, of an insane man who was seen wildly rushing about the house, from room to room, looking in cupboards and clothes-presses, crawling under beds, obviously searching for something. When questioned as to what he was so frantically looking for, he replied, "I am trying to find my self!" It is not as mad as it seems. I am not sure but that we who are not trying to find ourselves are after all more crazy still.

Old Burton, who wrote *The Anatomy of Melancholy*, well said:

> "Men look to their tools; a painter will wash his pencils; a smith will look to his hammer, anvil, and forge; a husbandman will mend his plow-irons and grind his hatchet, if it be dull; a musician will string and unstring his lute; only scholars neglect that instrument, their brains and spirits I mean, which they daily use."

Not scholars only, but all classes and conditions of men are guilty of this strange insanity. If the Duke of Westminster should offer to transfer to us his estates, we would rush with all conceivable speed to acquire our new potential possessions. We would go as with wings of an aeroplane to get the transaction accomplished before anything could occur to keep us from entering into our fortune. But here we are already within reach of a vastly better possession, of which we are strangely negligent. If it came to a choice between himself and his outward possessions, this duke who owns so much would not hesitate a minute which to prefer. If in a crisis of illness he could save himself by surrender of his goods, they would instantly go. "Give me health and a day," Emerson said, "and I will make the pomp of emperors ridiculous."

What we would do in a crisis we often fail to do when no crisis confronts us, and it is a fact that too often we miss and even squander that better possession, ourselves. The best way to win it and enjoy it is to cultivate those inner experiences and endowments which make us independent of external fortune. All Christ's beatitudes attach to some inherent quality of life itself. The meek, the merciful, the pure, are "happy," not because the external world conforms to their wishes, but because they have resources of life within themselves and have entered upon a way of life which continually opens out into more life and richer life. They have found a kind of Canaan that "comes" in continuous instalments.

One of the simplest ways to heighten the total value of life is to form a habit of appreciating the world we have here and now. It presents occasional inconveniences, no doubt, but think of the amazing donations which come to us: the tilting of the earth's axis twenty-three and a half degrees to the ecliptic by which contrivance we have our seasons; the fact that the proportion of earth and water is just right to give us a fine balance of rain and sunshine; the extraordinary way in which the entire universe submits to our mathematics so that every movement of matter and every vibration of ether conforms to laws which we formulate; the accumulation and storage of fuel and motor power, with the prospect of even greater resources of energy to be had from the unoccupied space surrounding the earth. Then, again, it cannot be a matter of unconcern that there is such a wealth of beauty lavished upon us everywhere, waiting for us to enjoy it. There is here a strange fit between the outer and the inner. The more one draws upon the beauty of the world and enjoys it, so much the more does he increase his capacity to discover and enjoy beauty. Coal and oil may become exhausted, but beauty is inexhaustible. The only trouble is that we are so limited in our range of appreciation of it. We turn to cheaper values and miss so much of this free gift of loveliness.

Greater still should be our resources of love and friendship. Nothing could be stranger or more wonderful than that in a world where struggle for existence is the law this other trait should have emerged. It is easy to explain selfishness; love is the mystery. Love forgets itself; it scorns double-entry bookkeeping; it gives, it bestows, it shares, it sacrifices without asking whether anything is coming back. And it turns out to be a fact that nothing else so enhances and increases the value of this "better possession which is ourselves."

Even more wonderful, if that is possible, is the way we are formed and contrived to have intercourse with the Eternal. With all our material furnishings we strangely open out into the infinite and partake of a spiritual nature. God has set eternity in our hearts. We cannot win this better possession nor hold it permanently unless we exercise these spiritual capacities, which expand our being and add the richest qualities of life. "Thou hast made us for thyself," Augustine acknowledged in his great prayer at the opening of the *Confessions* and "we are restless until we find thee as our true rest." It is as true now as in the fourth century. Barns and houses, lands and stocks, mortgages and bonds, do not constitute life unless one learns how to win and possess his soul and to keep that best of all possessions—himself.

III
THE GREATEST RIVALRIES OF LIFE

"After experience had taught me that all things which are encountered in human life are vain and futile.... I at length determined to inquire if there was anything which was a true good." Those are the words of a great philosopher who says that he found himself "led by the hand up to the highest blessedness."

Not everybody finds the choice of ends so easy as Spinoza did; not all of us are carried along into sustained and unmistakable blessedness. Life is full of rivalries which tend to divide our interest and to dissipate our attention. We wake up, perhaps, with surprise to discover that we are being carried, by the hand or by the hair, straight away from "the highest blessedness." Not seldom the sternest tragedies of human life are occasioned by success. Failure overtaking one in his aim will often shake him awake and make him see that he was pursuing an end in sharp rivalry with his highest good. But success often dulls the vision for other issues and gives one the specious confidence that he is on the right track and "all's well."

Christ has a vivid parable which touches upon the rivalries of life. It is the story of a great feast to which many guests are invited. When the critical moment for the dinner comes the other rivalries begin to operate. One man, attracted by his possessions, "begs off," to use the graphic phrase of the original. Another, occupied with the complex interests of business and busy with the affairs of trade, prays to be excused. A third is immersed in the joys and responsibilities of married life and he abruptly dispatches his "regrets." It was not that they were unconcerned about the sumptuous feast, but that they were carried along by rival interests.

The feast in this parable plainly stands for the "true good," the "highest blessedness" of life. It symbolizes the goal and crown of life, the full realization of our best human possibilities, the attainment of that for which we were made aspiring beings. The invitation is a mark of amazing grace and the recipient of it has the clearest evidence that the feast would satisfy him. But there are the other things with their rival attractions! Possessions and business and domestic life pull us in a contrary direction. We send our cards of regret and beg off from the great feast.

The real mistake lies in treating these things as rivals. If we only knew it, an affirmative response to the great invitation of life would prepare us for all the other things and would heighten the value of all we own, of all we do, and of all we love. Salvation is not some remote and ghostly thing that has to do with another world. It is the infusion of new life and power into all the concerns and affairs of this present world where we are. It means, as Christ said, receiving "a hundredfold now in this time, houses and brethren, and sisters, and mothers, and children, and lands, with persecutions; and in the world to come eternal life."

Nothing could be a more mistaken way than to regard human love as a rival to the highest of all relations, the love of the soul for God. One of the medieval saints said: "God brooks no rival"; but that phrase shows that the saint was caught napping, and in any case did not quite understand what love is. The way up to the highest love is not to be found by turning away from those experiences which give us training and preparation for the highest; but rather it is found in and through the experience of loving some person who, however imperfectly, is a revelation of the beauty and divineness of love. Not by some sheer leap from the earth does the soul arrive at its height of blessedness, but by steps and stages, by processes which bring illumination and richness of life. The man who has married a wife will do well to say when he answers the great invitation: "I have just married a wife and therefore I am peculiarly glad to come to thy feast, since fellowship with thee will make my love more real and true as that in turn will enable me to rise to a more genuine appreciation of thy love."

The same is true of houses and lands, of business and trade. There is no necessary rivalry here. Religion does not rob us of earthly interests, it does not strip us of the good things of this world. It only corrects our perspective and enables us to see the true scale of values. The trivial and fragmentary things of the world no longer absorb us. We refuse now to allow them to own us and drive us, or drag us. We see things steadily and we see them whole. We discover through our higher contacts and inspirations how to flood light back upon our occupations and upon the things we own, and how to make these subordinate things minister to the higher functions and attitudes of life. We get not some other world, but this world here and now transmuted and raised a little nearer to the ideal and perfect world of our hopes and dreams. We get it back item for item increased a hundredfold, raised to a higher spiritual level. The wise owner of property and the intelligent man of affairs will not beg off when the great invitation comes to him. He will say: "I have just come into possession of a piece of land, I have bought five yoke of oxen, and therefore I want to come to thy divine feast so that I may learn how to turn all I possess into the channels of real service and to make these things which thou hast given me help me find the way to the highest joy and blessedness of life."

CHAPTER VI
AGENCIES OF CONSTRUCTION

I
THE CHURCH OF THE LIVING GOD

We have all been asking, "What is the matter with the Church? Why is it so weak and ineffective? Why does it exercise such a feeble influence in the world to-day? Why do men care so little for its message and its mission?" There are no doubt many answers to these questions, but one answer concerns us here. It is this: We who compose the Church do not sufficiently realize that God is a living God and that the Church is intended to be the living body through which he works in the world and through which he reveals himself. We think of him as far away in space and remote in time, a God who created once and who worked wonders in ancient times long past, but we do not, as we should, vividly think of him as a living reality, as near to us as the air is to the flying bird or the water to the swimming fish. We suppose that the Church is made up of just people, and is a human convenience for getting things done in the world. We do not see as we should that it is meant to be both divine and human and that it never is properly a Church unless God lives in it, reveals himself by means of it and works his spiritual work in the world through it.

This truth of the real Presence breaks through many of Christ's great sayings and was one of the most evident features of the experience of the early Church. "Wherever in all the world two or three shall gather in my name there am I in the midst of them." "Lo, I am with you always, even unto the end of the world." "Wherever there is one alone," according to the newly found "saying" of Jesus, "I am with him. Raise the stone and there thou shalt find me; cleave the wood and there am I."

Not once alone was the early Church invaded by a life and power from beyond itself as at Pentecost. The consciousness which characterized this "upper room" experience was repeated in some degree wherever a Church of the living God came into existence, as "a tiny island in a sea of surrounding paganism." To belong to the Church meant to St. Paul to be "joined to the Lord in one spirit," while the Church itself in his great phrase is the body of Christ and each individual a member in particular of that body.

What a difference it would make if we could rise to the height of St. Paul's expectation and be actually "builded together for an habitation of God through the Spirit!" We try plenty of other expedients. We popularize our message; we take up fads; we adjust as far as we can to the tendencies of the time; but only one thing really works after all and that is having the Church become the organ of the living God, and having it "charged" with what Paul so often calls the power of God—"the power that worketh in us."

I saw a car wheel recently that had been running many miles with the brake clamped tight against it. It was white hot and it glowed with heat and light until it seemed almost transparent in its extraordinary luminosity. Those Christians in the upper room at Pentecost were baptized with fire so that the whole personality of each of them was glowing with heat and light, for the fire had gone all through them. They suddenly became conscious that their divine Leader who was no longer visible with them had become an invisible presence and a living power working through them. It is no wonder that all Jerusalem and its multitudinous sojourners were at once awakened to the fact that something novel had happened.

Our controversies which have divided us have been controversies about things out at the periphery, not about realities at the heart and center. We disagree about baptism, and we are at variance over problems of organization, ministry, and ordination, but the thing that really matters is the depth of conviction, consciousness of God, certainty of communion and fellowship with the Spirit. These experiences unite and never divide.

There is after all, in spite of all our gaps and chasms, only one Church. It is the Church of the living God. We are named with many names. We bear the sign of a particular denomination, but if we belong truly to the Church, then we belong to the great Church of the living God. It is built upon the foundation of the apostles and prophets, Jesus Christ himself being the chief cornerstone, in whom the building, fitly framed together, grows into an holy temple in the Lord. This is "the blessed community," the living, expanding fellowship of vital faith, and it has the promise of the future, whether conferences on "faith and order" succeed or not, because it is the Church of the living God.

II
THE NURSERY OF SPIRITUAL LIFE

We are coming more and more to realize that religion attaches to the simple, elemental aspects of our human life. We shall not look for it in a few rare, exalted, and so-called "sacred" aspects of life, separated off from the rest of life and raised to a place apart. Religion to be real and vital must be rooted in life itself and it must express itself through the whole life. It should begin, where all effective education must begin, in the home, which should be the nursery of spiritual life.

The Christian home is the highest product of civilization; in fact there is nothing that can be called civilization where the home is absent. The savage is on his way out of savagery as soon as he can create a home and make family life at all sacred. The real horror of the "slums" in our great cities is that there are no homes there, but human beings crowded indiscriminately into one room. It is the real trouble with the "poor whites" whether in the South or in the North that they have failed to preserve the home as a sacred center of life.

One of the first services of the foreign missionary is to help to establish homes among the people whom he hopes to Christianize. In short, the home is the true unit of society. It determines what the individual shall be; it shapes the social life; it makes the Church possible; it is the basis of the state and nation. A society of mere individual units is inconceivable. Men and women, each for self, and with no holy center for family life, could never compose either a Church or a State.

Christianity has created the home as we know it, and that is its highest service to the world, for the kingdom of heaven would be realized if the Christian home were universal. The mother's knee is still the holiest place in the world; and the home life determines more than all influences combined what the destiny of the boy or girl shall be. The formation of disposition and early habits of thought and manner as well as the fundamental emotions and sentiments do more to shape and fix the permanent character than do any other forces in the world.

We may well rejoice in the power of the Sunday school, the Christian ministry, the secular school, the college, the university; but all together they do not measure up to the power of the homes which are silently, gradually determining the future lives of those who will compose the Sunday school, the Church, the school, and the college.

The woman who is successful in making a true home, where peace and love dwell, in which the children whom God gives her feel the sacredness and holy meaning of life, where her husband renews his strength for the struggles and activities of his life, and in which all unite to promote the happiness and highest welfare of each other—that woman has won the best crown there is in this life, and she has served the world in a very high degree. The union of man and woman for the creation of a home breathing an atmosphere of love is Christ's best parable of the highest possible spiritual union where the soul is the bride and he is the Eternal Bridegroom, and they are one.

It seems strange that these vital matters are so little emphasized or regarded. Few things in fact are more ominous than the signs of the disintegration of the home as a nursery of spiritual life. We can, perhaps, weather catastrophes which may break down many of our ancient customs and even obliterate some of the institutions which now seem essential to civilization; but the home is a fundamental necessity for true spiritual nurture and culture, and if it does not perform its function the world will drift on toward unspeakable moral disasters.

III
THE DEMOCRACY WE AIM AT

Democracy was in an earlier period only a political aim; it has now become a deep religious issue. It must be discussed not only in caucuses and conventions, but in churches as well. For a century and a quarter "democracy" has been a great human battle word, and battle words never have very exact definitions. It has all the time been charged with explosive forces, and it has produced a kind of magic spell on men's minds during this long transitional period. But the word democracy has, throughout this time, remained fluid and ill-defined—sometimes expressing the loftiest aspirations and sometimes serving the coarse demagogue in his pursuit of selfish ends.

The goal or aim of the early struggle after democracy was the overthrow of human inequalities. Men were thought of in terms of individual units, and the units were declared to be intrinsically equal. The contention was made that they all had, or ought to have, the same rights and privileges. This equality-note has, too, dominated the social and economic struggles of the last seventy-five years. The focus has been centered upon rights and privileges. Men have been thought of, all along, as individual units, and the goal has been conceived in political and economic terms. Democracy is still supposed, in many quarters, to be an organization of society in which the units have equal political rights. Much of the talk concerning democracy is still in terms of privileges. It is a striving to secure opportunities and chances. The aim is the attainment of a social order in which guarantee is given to every individual that he shall have his full economic and political rights.

I would not, in the least, belittle the importance of these claims, or underestimate the human gains which have been made thus far in the direction of greater equality and larger freedom. But these achievements, however valuable, are not enough. They can only form the base from which to start the drive for a more genuine and adequate type of democracy. At its best this scheme of "equality" is abstract and superficial. Nobody will ever be satisfied with an achievement of flat equality. Persons can never be reduced to homogeneous units. There are individual differences woven into the very fiber of human life, and no type of democracy can ever satisfy men like us until it gets beyond this artificial scheme and learns to deal with the problem in more adequate fashion.

A genuinely Christian democracy such as the religious soul is after can not be conceived in economic terms, nor can it be content with social units of equality or sameness. We want a democracy that is vitally and spiritually conceived, which recognizes and safeguards the irreducible uniqueness of every member of the social whole. This means that we can not deal with personal life in terms of external behavior. We can not think of society as an aggregation of units possessing individual rights and privileges. We shall no longer be satisfied to regard persons as beings possessing utilitarian value or made for economic uses. We shall forever transcend the instrumental idea. We shall begin rather with the inalienable fact of spiritual worth as the central feature of the personal life. This would mean that every person, however humble or limited in scope or range, has divine possibilities to be realized; is not a "thing" to be used and exploited, but a spiritual creation to be expanded until its true nature is revealed. The democracy I want will treat every human person as a unique, sacred, and indispensable member of a spiritual whole, a whole which remains imperfect if even one of its "little ones" is missing; and its fundamental axiom will be the liberation and realization of the inner life which is potential in every member of the human race.

On the economic and equality level we never reach the true conception of personal life. Men are thought of as units having desires, needs, and wants to be satisfied. We are, on this basis, aiming to achieve a condition in which the desires, wants, and needs are well met, in which each individual contributes his share of supplies to the common stock of economic values, and receives in turn his equitable amount. I am dealing, on the other hand, with a way of life which begins and ends, not with a material value-concept at all, but rather with a central faith in the intrinsic worth and infinite spiritual possibilities of every person in the social organism—a democracy of spiritual agents.

It is true, no doubt, as Shylock said, that we all have "eyes, hands, organs, dimensions, senses, affections, passions," are "subject to diseases," and "warmed and cooled by summer and winter." "If you prick us we bleed, if you tickle us we laugh, if you poison us we die," and so on. We do surely have wants and needs. We must consider values. We must have food and clothes and houses. We must have some fair share of the earth and its privileges. But that is only the basement and foundation of real living, and we want a democracy that is supremely concerned with the development of personality and with the spiritual organization of society. We shall not make our estimates of persons on a basis of their uses, or on the ground of their behavior as animal beings; we shall live and work, if we are Christ's disciples, in the faith that man is essentially a spiritual being, in a world which is essentially spiritual, and that we are committed to the task of awakening a like faith in others and of helping realize an organic solidarity of persons who practice this faith. Our rule of life would be something like the following: to act everywhere and always as though we knew that we are members of a spiritual community, each one possessed of infinite worth, of irreducible uniqueness, and indispensable to the spiritual unity of the whole—a community that is being continually enlarged by the faith and action of those who now compose it, and so in some measure being formed by our human effort to achieve a divine ideal.

The most important service we can render our fellow men is to awaken in them a real faith in their own spiritual nature and in their own potential energies, and to set them to the task of building the ideal democracy in which personality is treated as sacred and held safe from violation, infringement, or exploitation, and, more than that, in which we altogether respect the worth and the divine hopes inherent in our being as men.

IV
THE ESSENTIAL TRUTH OF CHRISTIANITY

There are few questions more difficult to answer than the question, What is Christianity? Every attempt to answer it reveals the peculiar focus of interest in the mind of the writer, but it leaves the main question still asking for a new answer.

"Always it asketh, asketh," and each answer, to say the least, is inadequate. Harnack, Loisy, and Tolstoy have given three characteristic answers to the great question. Their books are touched with genius and will long continue to be read, but, like the other books, they, too, reveal the writers rather than solve the central problem.

One of the greatest difficulties about the whole matter is the difficulty of deciding where to look for the essential traits of Christianity. Are they to be found in the teaching of Jesus? Are they revealed in the message of St. Paul? Are they embodied in the Messianic hope? Are they exhibited in the primitive apostolic Church? Are they set forth in the great creeds of orthodoxy? Are they expressed in the imperial authoritative Church? Are they to be discovered in the Protestantism of the modern world? This catalogue of preliminary questions shows how complicated the subject really is. To start in on any one of these lines would be of necessity to arrive at a partial and one-sided answer.

Nowhere can we find pure and unalloyed Christianity; always we have it mixed and combined with something else, more or less foreign to it. The creeds contain a larger element of Greek philosophy than of the pure original gospel. The Messianic hope is far more Jewish than it is "Christian." The imperial authoritative Church is Christianity interpreted through the Roman genius for organization and merged and fused with the age-long faiths and customs of pagan peoples. Protestantism is an amazingly complex blend of ideas and ideals and everywhere interwoven with the long processes of history. Even this did not drop from the sky ready-made! Nor did St. Paul's message flash in upon him with the Damascus vision, as a pure heaven-presented truth. It proves to be a very difficult task to find one's way back to the pure, unalloyed teaching of Jesus, and, strangely enough, the moment one endeavors to constitute this by itself "Christianity," and undertakes to turn it into a set of commands and to make it a "new law," he ends with a dry legalism and not a vital, universal Christianity.

What, then, is Christianity? In answering this question we can not confine ourselves to the teaching and the work of Jesus. Important as it is to go "back to Jesus" that is not enough. We can not fully comprehend the meaning of Christianity until we take into account the fact that the invisible, resurrected Christ is the continuation through the ages of the same revelation begun in the life and teaching of Jesus. Galilee and Judea mark only one stage of the gospel, which is, in its fullness, an eternal gospel. The Christian revelation which came to light first in one Life—its master interpretation and incarnation—has since been going forward in a continuous and unbroken manifestation of Christ through many lives and through many groups and through the spiritual achievements of all those who have lived by him. Christianity is, thus, the revelation of God through personal life—God humanly revealed. St. Paul and the writer of the Fourth Gospel were the first to reach this profound insight into its fuller meaning, though it is plainly suggested in some of the sayings of Jesus and in the pentecostal experiences of the first Christians. It is the very heart of the Pauline and the Johannine Christianity. Important as is the backward look to Jesus in both these writers, the central emphasis is unmistakably upon the inward experience of the invisible, spiritual Christ. This is the expectation in the Fourth Gospel: Greater things than these shall ye do when the Spirit comes upon you. This is the mystery, the secret of the gospel, St. Paul says, Christ in you.

If this is the right clew, Christianity is not a new law, nor an institution, nor a creed, nor a body of doctrine, nor a millennial hope. It is a type of life, it is a way of living. The most essential thing about it is the fact of the incursion of God into human life, the revelation of the eternal in the midst of time, the new discovery which it brought of God's nature and character. We nowhere else come so close to the essential truth of Christianity as we do in the life and experience of Jesus. The life at every point floods over and transcends the teaching. He is the most complete and adequate exhibition of what I have called the incursion of God into human life, but even so he is the beginning, not the end, of the revelation of God through humanity—the Christ-revelation of God—and this Christ-revelation of God *is* God, so far as he is at all adequately known.

Some persons talk as though God were a kind of composite Being, got by adding up the God of the natural order, the God of the Old Testament, and the God as Father about whom Jesus taught. He is, according to this scheme, in some way a compound aggregate of infinite power, irresistible justice, and eternal love. Sometimes one "attribute" is predominant, and sometimes another, while in some mysterious way all the dissonant attributes get "reconciled." This is surely boggy ground to build upon.

Christianity is essentially, I should say, a unique revelation of God. Here for the first time the race discovers that God identifies himself with humanity, is in the stream of it, is suffering with us, is in moral conflict with sin and evil, is conquering through the travail and tragedy of finite persons, and is eternally, in mind and heart and will, a God of triumphing Love. No texts adequately "prove" this mighty truth. We cannot tie it down to "sayings," though there are "sayings" which declare it. The life of Jesus, the supreme decisions through which he expresses his purpose, the spirit which dominates him and guides his decisive actions, make the truth plain that God meant *that* to him and that his way of life revealed that kind of God.

Through all the fusions and confusions of history and through all the vagaries of man's tortuous course since the Church began to be built, Christ as eternal Spirit has gone on revealing this truth about God and demonstrating the victorious power of this way of life. The making of a kingdom of God in the world, the spread of the brother-spirit, the expansion of the love-method, the increase of coöperation, sympathy, and service, the continued incursion of the divine into the life of the human, these are the things now and always which indicate the vitality and progress of Christianity, and the uninterrupted revelation of God.

Always, in every period of history, the essential truth of Christianity must be revealed and expressed in and through a medium not altogether adapted to it. It is always living and working in a world more or less alien to it. It has at any stage only partially realized its ideal, and only achieved in a fragmentary way the goal toward which it is moving. It means endless conquest and ever fresh winning of unwon victories. It must be for us all a vision and a venture, it must be a thing of faith and forecast. At the same time it is, in a very real sense, experience and achievement. God *has* entered into humanity. Love has revealed its redeeming power. Grace is as much a reality as mountains are. The kingdom of God though not all in sight yet is, I believe, as sure as gravitation. The invisible, eternal Christ, living in the soul of man, revealing his will in moral and spiritual victories in personal lives, is, I am convinced, as genuine a fact as electricity is. But we shall see *all* that Christianity means only when the living totality of the revelation of God through humanity is complete.

CHAPTER VII
THE NEAR AND THE FAR

I
THINGS PRESENT AND THINGS TO COME

Anaxagoras said twenty-five hundred years ago that men are always cutting the world in two with a hatchet. William James, in one of his living phrases, says with the same import that everybody dichotomizes the cosmos. It is so. We all incline to bisect life into alternative possibilities. We split realities into opposing halves. We show a kind of fascination for an "either-or" selection. We are prone to use the principle of parsimony, and to be content with one side of a dilemma. History presents a multitude of dualistic pairs from which one was supposed to make his individual selection. There was the choice between this world and the next world; the here and the yonder; the flesh and the spirit; faith and reason; the sacred and the secular; the outward and the inward, and many more similar alternatives. This "either-or" method always leaves its trail of leanness behind. It makes life thin and narrow where it might be rich and broad, for in almost every case it is just as possible to have a whole as to have a half, to take both as to select an alternative. St. Paul found his Corinthians bisecting their spiritual lives and narrowing their interests to one or two possibilities. One of them would choose Paul as his representative of the truth and then see no value in the interpretation which Apollos had to give. Another attached himself to Apollos and missed all the rich contributions of Paul. Some of the "saints" of the Church selected Cephas as the only oracle, and they lost all the breadth which would have come to them had they been able to make a synthesis of the opposing aspects. St. Paul called them from their divided half to a completed whole. He told them that instead of "either-or" they could have both. "All things are yours; whether Paul or Apollos, or Cephas, or the world, or life, or death, or things present or things to come, all are yours; and ye are Christ's and Christ is God's." This is the method of synthesis. This is the substitution of wholes for halves, the proffer of both for an "either-or" alternative.

That last pair of alternatives is an interesting one, and many persons make their bisecting choice of life there. One well-known type of person focuses on the near, the here and now, the things present. Those who belong to this class propose to make hay while the sun shines. They glory in being practical. They have what doctors call myopia. They see only the near. Their lenses will not adjust for the remote. They believe in quick returns and bank upon practical results. Those of the other type have presbyopia, or far-sightedness. They are dedicated to the far-away, the remote, the yonder. They are pursuing rainbows and distant ideals. They are so eager for the millennium that they forget the problem of their street and of the present day. Browning has given us a picture of both these types:

"That low man seeks a little thing to do,
   Sees it and does it:
This high man, with a great thing to pursue,
   Dies ere he knows it.

That low man goes on adding one to one,
   His hundred's soon hit:
This high man, aiming at a million,
   Misses an unit."

Browning's sympathies are plainly with the "high man" who misses the unit, but it is one more case of unnecessary dichotomy. What we want is the discovery of a way to unite into one synthesis things present and things to come. We need to learn how to seize this narrow isthmus of a present and to enrich it with the momentous significance of past and future. Henry Bergson has been telling us that all rich moments of life are rich just because they roll up and accumulate the meaning of the past and because they are crowded with anticipations of the future. They are fused with memory and expectation, and one of these two factors is as important as the other. If either dies away the present becomes a useless half, like the divided parts of the child which Solomon proposed to bisect for the two contending mothers.

We are at one of those momentous ridges of time at the present moment. Some are so busy with the near and immediately practical that they cannot see the far vision of the world that is to be built. Others are so impressed with past issues that have become paramount, with the glorious memories of the blessed Monroe Doctrine, for instance, that they have no expectant eyes for the creation of an interrelated and unified world. Another group is so concerned with the social millennium that they discount the lessons of the past, the message of history, the wisdom of experience, and fly to the useless task of constructing abstract human paradises and dreams of a world-kingdom which could exist only in a realm where men had ceased to be men.

What we want is a synthesis of things present and things to come, a union of the practical, tested experience of life and the inspired vision of the prophet who sees unfolding the possibilities of human life raised to its fuller glory in Christ, the incarnation of the way of love, which always has worked, is working now, and always will work.

II
TWO TYPES OF MINISTRY

Most people like to be told what they already think. They enjoy hearing their own opinions and ideas promulgated, and no amens are so hearty as the ones which greet the reannouncement of views we have already held.

The natural result is that speakers are apt to give their hearers what they want. They take the line of least resistance and say what will arouse the enthusiasm of the people before them, and they get their quick reward. They are popular at once. There is a high tide of emotion as they proceed to tell what everybody present already thinks, and they soon find themselves in great demand.

The main trouble with such an easy ministry is that it isn't worth doing. It accomplishes next to nothing. It merely arouses a pleasurable emotion and leaves lives where they were before. And yet not quite where they were either, for the constant repetition of things we already believe dulls the mind and deadens the will and weakens rather than strengthens the power of life. It is an easy ministry both for speakers and hearers, but it is ominous for them both.

The prophet has a very different task. He cannot give people what they want. He is under an unescapable compulsion to give them what his soul believes to be true. He cannot take lines of least resistance; he must work straight up against the current. He cannot work for quick effects; he must slowly educate his people and compel them to see what they have not seen before. The amens are very slow to come to his words, and he cannot look for emotional thrills. He must risk all that is dear to himself, except the truth, as he sets himself to his task, and he is bound to tread lonely wine-presses before he can see of the travail of his soul and be satisfied.

Every age has these two types of ministry. They are both ancient and familiar. There are always persons who are satisfied to give what is wanted, who are glad to cater to popular taste, who like the quick returns. But there are, too, always a few souls to be found who volunteer for the harder task. They forego the amens and patiently teach men to see farther than they have seen before. Their first question is not, What do people want me to say? but, What is God's truth which to-day ought to be heard through me? and knowing that, they speak. They do not move their hearers as the other type does; they do not reach so many, and they miss the popular rewards—but they are compassed about by a great cloud of witnesses as they fight their battles for the truth, and they have their joy.

But this is not quite all there is to say. It is not possible to teach the new effectively without linking it up with the old. The wholly new is generally not true. New, fresh truth emerges out of ancient experience; it does not drop like a shooting star from the distant skies. The great prophets in all ages have lived close to the people. They have not had their "ear to the ground," to use a political phrase, but they have understood the human heart. They have lived in the great currents of life. They have heard the going in the mulberry trees, and have felt the breaking forth of the dawning light just because of their double union with men and God.

All sound pedagogy recognizes this principle. The good teacher knits the new material which he wishes learned on to the old and familiar. He takes his student forward by gradual stages, not by leaps and bounds, and he binds the known and unknown together by rational synthesis, not by some strange, foreign, magical glue. The more we wish to belong to the prophet-class and to raise our hearers to new and greater levels of truth and insight, the more we shall strive to understand the truth that has already been revealed, to saturate ourselves with it, to fuse and kindle our lives with those immense realities by which men in past ages have lived and conquered. So, and only so, can we go forward and take others forward with us to new experiences and to new discoveries of the light that never was on sea or land.

III
"WE HAVE SEEN HIS STAR"

Every time the Christmas anniversary returns, the heart renews its youthful joy in the thrilling stories of the nativity. We cannot be too thankful for the inspiration and poetry and imagination which touch and glorify every aspect of our religious faith. Some dull and leaden-minded pedants appear to think that the "real" Christ is the person we get when we take, for the construction of our figure, only those facts about him which can be rationalistically, historically, and critically verified. We are thus reduced to a few religious ideas, a little group of "sayings," a tiny body of events, which explain none of the immense results that followed. The real Christ, on the contrary, is this rich, wonderful, mysterious, baffling person whose life was vastly greater even than his deeds or his words, who aroused the wonder and imagination of all who came in contact with him, who touched everything with emotion, and fused religion forever with poetry and feeling. He, in a very true sense,

" ... touches all things common,
Till they rise to touch the spheres."

Not only over the manger, but over the entire story of his life, hovers the glory of the star. It is a life that will not stay down on the dull earth of mere fact; it always rises into the region of idealism and beauty. It always transcends the things of sight and touch. We have a religion which cannot be confined in a system of doctrine or a code of ethics; it partakes too intimately of life for that. It is, like its Founder, a full rounded reality, rich in inspiration and emotion and wonder, as well as in intellectual ideas and truth. When the star wanes and imagination falls away, and we hold in our thin hands only the husks of a dead system, the power of religion is over.

The same thing is true of the cross. Its power lies in the fullness and richness of the reality. We do not want to reduce it, but to raise it to its full meaning and glory as a way of complete life. The direction of present-day

Christianity is certainly not away from Calvary, but quite the opposite. The men who are in these days trying to deliver our religion from formalism and tradition find not less meaning in the cross than a former generation did, but vastly more. The atonement remains at the center, as it has always done, in vital Christianity. All attempts to reduce Christianity to a dry and bloodless system of philosophy, with the appeal of the heart left out, fail now as they have always failed. It is a Savior that men, tangled in their sins and their sorrows, still want—not merely a great thinker or a great teacher.

The Church has, no doubt, far too much neglected the idea of the kingdom of God as Christ expounded it in sermon and parable, and hosts of prominent Christians do not at all understand what this great, central teaching of the Master meant then and means now. His transforming revelation of the nature of God has, too, been missed by multitudes, who still hold Jewish rather than Christian conceptions of God. But patient study of the gospel is slowly forcing these ideas into the thought of men everywhere, and books abound now which make his teaching clear and luminous.

What is needed above everything else now is that we shall not lose any of our vision of Christ as Savior, and that we shall live our lives in his presence. It is through the cross that we touch closest to the Savior-heart, and it is here that we feel our lives most powerfully moved by the certainty of his divine nature. Arguments may fail, but one who looks steadily at this voluntary Sufferer, giving himself for us, will cry out, with one of old, "My Lord and my God."

Nothing short of that will do, I believe, if Christianity is to remain a saving religion. Good men have died in all ages; great teachers have again and again gone to their deaths in behalf of their truth or out of love for their disciples. It touches us as we read of their bravery and their loyalty, but we do not and we cannot build a world-saving religion upon them. Christ is different! We feel that in him the veil is lifted and we are face to face with God. When we hear with our hearts the words, "In the world ye shall have tribulation; but fear not, for I have overcome the world," we feel that we are hearing the triumph of God in the midst of suffering—we are hearing of an eternal triumph. Christ can not be for us less than God manifested here in a world of time and space and finiteness, doing in time what God does in eternity—suffering over sin, entering vicariously into the tragedy of evil, and triumphing while he treads the winepress. No one has fathomed the awfulness of sin, until, in some sense, he feels that his sin makes God suffer, that it crucifies him afresh. If Christ is God revealed in time—made visible and vocal to men—then, through the cross, we shall discover that we are not to think of God henceforth as Sovereign—not a Being yonder, enjoying his royal splendor. We must think of him all the time in terms of Christ. He is an eternal Lover of our hearts. We pierce him with our sins; we wound him with our wickedness. He suffers, as mothers who love suffer, and he enters vicariously into all the tragic deeps of our lives, striving to bring us home to him. Jan Ruysbroeck says:

"You must love the Love which loves you everlastingly, and if you hold fast by his love, he remakes you by his Spirit, and then joy is yours. The Spirit of God breathes into you, and you breathe it out in rest and joy and love. This is eternal life, just as in our mortal life we breathe out the air that is in us and breathe in fresh air."

CHAPTER VIII
THE LIGHT-FRINGED MYSTERY

I
THE RELIGIOUS SIGNIFICANCE OF DEATH

The Greeks had their story of Tithonus, a deeply significant myth of a man who could not die, but who grew ever older and more decrepit until the tragedy became unendurable and he envied those "happy men that have the power to die." Methuselah's biography is brief and compact, but it is full of pathos: "He lived nine hundred and sixty-nine years and he died." There was nothing more to add. Somebody has invented a radium motor which strikes a little bell every second and is warranted to go on doing that for thirty thousand years. The Methuselah monotony and tedium seem much like that thin *seriatim* row of items. It just goes on with no novelty and no cumulation, and finally the one relieving novelty is introduced—"he died." What a happy fact it was! The wandering Jew stands out in imaginative fiction as one of the saddest of all men—a being who endlessly goes on. The angel of death seems a gentle, gracious messenger when one thinks of the prospect of unending life, going on in a one-dimensional series, with no new values and no fresh powers of expansion. To many persons the idea of heaven is simply an expanded Methuselah biography.

Biologists have completely reversed the theory that death is an enemy. It has long ago taken its place in the system of teleology, among "the things that are for us." Death has, beyond question, and has had, "a natural utility." It has played an important *rôle* in raising life from the low unicellular type to the rich complex forms of higher organisms, from "the amœba that never dies of old age" to the new dynasty of beings that have greater range and scope, but which nevertheless do die. Edwin Arnold in his striking essay on *Death* says: "The lowest living thing, the Protamœba, has obviously never died! It is a formless film of protoplasm, which multiplies by simple division; and the specimen under any microscope derives, and must derive, in unbroken existence from the amœba which moved and fed forty æons ago. The slime of our nearest puddle lived before the Alps were made!" Methuselah was a mere child in a perambulator compared to an amœba.

In cases where the continued process of cell-division produced a lowered and weakened type of amœba a rudimentary form of union of cells took place, which resulted in raising the entire level of life and eventually carried the biological order up to wholly new possibilities. So that the threatened approach of death was met with an increase of life. "It is more probable that death is a consequence of life," says the famous biologist, Edward Cope, "rather than that the living is a product of the non-living."[2]

But in any case the testimony of biology can give us little help. Even if death has had a function in the process of evolution, as seems likely, that in no way eases the situation when the staggering blow falls into our precious circle and removes from it an intimate personal life that was indispensable to us. It is poor, cold comfort to be told that death has assisted through the long æons in the slow process of heightening the entire scale of life, if there is nothing more to say regarding the future of this dear one whose frail bark has now gone to wreck. We must somehow rise above the level of brute facts and discover some spiritual significance which death has revealed, before we can arrive at any source of comfort. We are all agreed with Shakespeare's Claudio that "'tis too horrible" to think of death as a sheer terminus:

> " ... to die and go we know not where;
> To lie in cold obstruction, and to rot;
> This sensible warm motion to become
> A kneaded clod; and the delighted spirit
> To bathe in fiery floods, or to reside
> In thrilling regions of rock-ribbed ice;
> To be imprisoned in the viewless winds,
> And blown with restless violence round about
> The pendent world."

Death has undoubtedly brought to consciousness, as has perhaps no other experience, the deeper meaning and significance of personal life. This and not its biological function is what concerns us now. It has been said that "freedom," so far as it is achieved, "is the main achievement of man in the past."[3] I should be inclined rather to hold that man's main achievement on the planet so far has been to discover that personal life reveals within itself an absolute value and possesses unmistakable capacity to transcend the finite and temporal, an experience which makes freedom possible. I believe death has ministered more than any other single fact that confronts us in bringing those truths to clear consciousness. We cannot, of course, dissociate death and separate it from pain, suffering, struggle and danger, which are essentially bound up with it. If the world were to be freed completely from death it would at once *ipso facto* be freed from the danger of it and by the same altered condition struggle would to a large degree be eliminated, and likewise those other great tests of life—pain and suffering, which culminate in death. These things are all "perilous incidents" of finiteness, but of a finiteness which transcends itself and is allied to something beyond itself. To eliminate these things would be to miss the discovery of this strange finite-infinite nature of ours which makes life such a venture and so full of mystery and wonder. If we had been only naturalistic beings, curious bits of the earth's crust merely capable of recording the empirical facts as they occurred, death would have taken an unimportant place as one more event in a successive series of phenomena. Built as we are, however, with a beyond within ourselves, the fact of mutability and mortality has occasioned a transformation of our entire estimate of life and has led us by the hand to a Pisgah view which we should never have got if there had been no invasion of death into our world.

"It is a venerable commonplace," as Professor Schiller of Oxford has said, "that among the melancholy prerogatives which distinguish man from the other animals and bestow a deeper significance on human life is the fact that man alone is aware of the doom that terminates his earthly existence, and on this account lives a more spiritual life, in the ineffable consciousness of the 'sword of Damocles' which overshadows him and weights his lightest action with gigantic import. Nay, more; stimulated by the ineluctable necessity of facing death, and of living so as to face it with fortitude, man has not abandoned himself to nerveless inaction, to pusillanimous despair; he has conceived the thought, he has cherished the hope, he has embraced the belief, of a life beyond the grave, and opened his soul to the religions which baulk the king of terrors of his victims and defraud him of his victory. Thus, the fear of death has been redeemed, and ennobled by the consoling belief in immortality, a belief from which none are base enough to withhold their moral homage, even though the debility of mortal knowledge may debar a few from a full acceptance of its promise."[4]

The early animistic views of survival, which were the first forecasts of a life beyond, were due not so much to the consciousness of the moral grandeur of life as to *actual experiences* which gave to primitive man a confident assurance of some form of life after the death of the body. Dreams had an important part in leading man to this naïve and yet momentous discovery. In a world which had no established criterion of "reality," the experiences of vivid dreams were taken to be as real as any other experiences, and in these dreams the dreamer often found his dead ancestors and friends and tribesmen once more present with him, active in the chase or the fight and as real as ever they were in life. Trance, hallucination, telepathy, mediumship, possession, are not new phenomena; they are very primitive and ancient. These things are as old as smiling and weeping. These psychic experiences had their part to play also in giving the early races their belief that the dead person still existed though in an altered and attenuated form as an *animus* or "spirit" or "shade." This empirical view of survival, built on actual experiences, was more or less incapable of advance. No further knowledge could be acquired and the constructions fashioned by imagination, in reference to "the scenery and circumstance" of the departed soul, could satisfy only an uncritical mind. These constructions were, too, often crude and bizarre, and tended, in the hands of priests, to hamper man's moral development rather than to further it. But in any case man had made the momentous guess that death did not utterly end him or his career. Poor and thin as this dimly conceived future world of primitive man's hope may have been, the psychological effect of the hope was by no means negligible. Professor Shaler of Harvard was probably speaking truly when he wrote:

"If we should seek some one mark, which in the intellectual advance from the brutes to man, might denote the passage to the human side, we might well find it in the moment when it dawned upon the nascent man that death was a mystery which he had in his turn to meet. From the time when man began to face death to the present stage of his development there has been a continuous struggle between the motives of personal fear on the one hand, and valor on the other. That of fear has been constantly aided by the work of the imagination. For one fact of danger there have been scores of fancied risks to come from the unseen world. Against this great host of imaginary ills, which tended utterly to bear men down, they had but one helper—their spirit of valiant self-sacrifice for the good of their family, their clan, their state, their race, or, in the climax, for the Infinite above."[5]

It marked a still greater intellectual advance when primitive man came to the immense conclusion not only that death was a mystery which he in turn must meet, but that he was a being that would survive death.

It is, however, in another field that we must look for the most important spiritual results from the contemplation of death, that is in what we may call the field of spiritual values. I have already contended that man's greatest discovery was his discovery of the absolute value of moral personality. Of course, it came fairly late in the development of the race and by no means has everybody made it yet! But at any rate there came a time somewhere in the process of history when man did discover a beyond within himself, a greater inclusive self present within his own fragmentary, finite spirit, revealed as a passion for perfection not yet attained or experienced, a prophesying consciousness of eternity within his often baffled and defeated temporal life. No one has expressed the fact of this inner beyond within us better than old Sir Thomas Browne did in the seventeenth century: "We are men and we know not how; there is something in us that can be without us and will be after us, though it is strange that it hath no history of what it was before us, nor can tell how it entered in us.... There is surely a piece of Divinity in us, something that was before the elements and owes not homage unto the Sun."

The sublimity and grandeur revealed in nature, the majesty of mountains, the might of seas, the mystery of the ocean, the glory of the sun and stars, the awe inspired by the thunderstorm, awakened man's own spirit and made him dimly conscious of a kindred grandeur in his own answering soul. The greatest step of all was taken when man awoke to the meaning and value of love. In some dim sense love preceded the emergence of man. The evolution of a mother and of a father, as Drummond showed, began far back in forms of life below man. But the type of love which transcends instinct, which is raised above sex-assertion, and is transmuted into an unselfish appreciation of the beauty and worth of personal character—that type of love is one of the most wonderful flowers that has yet blossomed on our

Igdrasil tree of life and it was late and slow to come, like flowers on the century-plant.

When death broke in and separated those who loved in this great fashion the whole problem of death at once became an urgent one. In fact death received *attention* in proportion as the higher values of life began to be realized. Walt Whitman's fiery outburst reveals clearly his estimate of the worth of personality. "If rats and maggots end us, then alarum! for we are betrayed"—he might have said "if microbes end us." Emerson's poignant outcry of soul is found in his greatest poem—"Threnody":

"There's not a sparrow or a wren,
There's not a blade of autumn grain,
Which the four seasons do not tend
And tides of life and increase lend;
And every chick of every bird,
And weed and rock-moss is preferred.
O ostrich-like forgetfulness!
O loss of larger in the less!
Was there no star that could be sent,
No watcher in the firmament,
No angel from the countless host
That loiters round the crystal coast,
Could stoop to heal that only child,
Nature's sweet marvel undefiled,
And keep the blossom of the earth,
Which all her harvests were not worth?"

No such high revolt of spirit was occasioned so long as death was a mere biological event, terminating one life to give room for another. This cry of soul means the discovery of the infinite preciousness of personal life. The mind now turns in on itself and takes a new account of its stock, and as a result man began to solve the problem of death in an enlarged way. He was no longer satisfied with a form of survival based upon his experiences in dreams, trance and hallucination; he came to feel that he must have a destiny which fitted his spiritual worth as a man. He finds within himself intimation of powers and possibilities beyond those required for the struggle of life here. He feels by that same insight which carries him out beyond the seen to a rational faith in the unseen that is necessary to complete it, that this little arc of earthly life with its revelations of spiritual value and its transcendent prophecies of more must find fulfillment somewhere in a form of life that rounds it out full circle.

The argument does not build on a passion of desire, as some doubters have said. We do not assume immortality just because we want it. It rests upon the moral consistency of the universe, upon the trustworthy character of the eternal nature of things. The moral values which are revealed in fully developed personality are certainly as *real*, as much a fact of the universe, as are the tides or the orbits of planets. If we can count upon the continuity of these occurrences and upon our predictions of them, just as surely can we count on the consistency of the universe in reference to spiritual values. If there is conservation of matter there is at least as good ground for affirming conservation of moral values. If biological life can pass over the slender bridge of a microscopic germ-plasm and can carry with itself over that feeble bridge the traces of habit and feature, the curve of nose and the emotional tone of some far-off dead ancestor, and all the heredity gains of the past, may we not count upon the permanence of that in us which allies us to that infinite Spirit who is even now the invisible environment of all we see and touch?

It is not a matter of reward or of "wages" that concerns us. It is not "happy isles" or care-free "Edens" that we seek, not "golden streets" and endless comfort to make up for the stress and toil of the lean years here below. We want to find the whole of ourselves, we ask the privilege of seeing this fragmentary being of ours unfold into the full expression of its gifts and powers. The new period may be even more strenuous and hazardous than this one has been—still we want the venture. We ask for the culminating acts that will complete the drama, so far only fairly begun. It must be not a mere serial, or straight line, existence; it must be the opening out and expansion of the possibilities which we feel within ourselves—new dimensions, please God.

I am not wrong, I am sure, in claiming that this postulate, this rational faith in the conservation of values, is an asset which death has revealed to the race. The shock of death has always made love appear a greater thing than we knew before the baffling crisis came upon us. It has, too, by the same shock of contrast, awakened man to the full comprehension of the moral sublimity of the good life. Kant maintained that the sense of the sublime is due to the fact that when we are confronted with the supreme powers of nature we then become aware of something unfathomable in ourselves, and feel that we are superior to the might of the storm, or the mountain or the cataract. Nowhere is this truer than when man—man in his full, rich powers—is confronted by death. Instead of cringing in fear, he rises to an unaccustomed height of greatness and is utterly superior to death and aware of some quality of being in himself which death cannot touch. It is just then in that moment of seeming disaster and dissolution that a brave, good man is most triumphant and ready to burn all bridges behind him in his great adventure. Mrs. Browning, all her life an invalid, says about this so-called gigantic enemy: "I cannot look on the earthside of death. When I look deathwards I look over death and upwards." Her husband, who was "ever a fighter," has this way of announcing the triumph:

"And then as, 'mid the dark, a gleam
Of yet another morning breaks,
   And like the hand which ends a dream,
Death, with the might of his sunbeam,
Touches the flesh and the soul awakes."[6]

Here is the testimony of a French soldier who writes at a moment when death is close beside him: "I had often known the joy of seeing a spring come like this, but never before had I been given the power of living in every instant. So it is that one wins, without the help of any science, a vague but indisputable intuition of the Absolute.... These are hours of such beauty that he who embraces them knows not what death means."

Having come upon the higher values of personal life which death has forced upon us we can never again, as men, be satisfied with such facts of survival as may come to light through dreams, hallucinations, telepathy and mediums, or in fact through any empirical experiences. Even if the evidence were vastly greater than it is for some form of animistic survival, it would fall far short of our moral and spiritual demands. We already have some intimations in us of "the power of an endless life," and we seek for a chance to bring it full into play, for the "heavenly period" to "perfect the earthen," for an ampler life that will reveal what we have all the time *meant* life to be.

Winifred Kirkland in *The New Death* well says: "The New Death, *i.e.*, the new view of death, is the perception of our mortal end as the mere portal of an eternal progression and the immediate result is the consecration of all living.... It is a new illumination, a New Death, when dying can be the greatest inspiration of our everyday energy, the strongest impulse toward daily joy."

II
THE NEW BORN OUT OF THE OLD

Walking across the fields in the spring I found the empty shell of a bird's egg. The tiny bird that once was in it was lying still and happy under its mother's wings, or was chirping its new-born song from the limb of a nearby tree, or was trying its new-found wings on the buoyant air. The empty shell was utterly worthless, a mere plaything for the wind. The miracle of life that had stirred within it and had used it for its shelter had gone on and left it deserted. There is a fine proverb which says, "God empties the nest by hatching out the eggs," and the world is full of this gentle, silent, divine method of abolishing the old by setting free to higher ends all that was true and living in it.

> "To-day I saw the dragon-fly
> Come from the wells where he did lie.
> An inner impulse rent the veil
> Of his old husk: from head to tail
> Came out clear plates of sapphire mail.
> He dried his wings: like gauze they grew;
> Through crofts and pastures wet with dew
> A living flash of light he flew."

In the water below, the "old husk" lay empty and useless, while the bright-colored living thing found its freedom in the invisible air. I never go to a funeral without thinking of this miracle of transformation which brings the bird out of the egg, the flower out of the seed, the dragon-fly out of its water-larva. In his own mysterious way God has emptied the nest by the hatching method, and all that was excellent, lovable, and permanent in the one we loved has found itself in the realm for which it was fitted. The body is only the empty shell, the shattered seed, the old husk, which the silent forces of nature will slowly turn back again into its original elements, to use over again for its myriad processes of building:

> "And from his ashes may be made
> The violet of his native land."

Those who treasure up the outworn dust and ashes, who make their thoughts center about the empty shell, are failing to read aright the deeper fact, which life everywhere is trying to utter, that that which belongs in the higher sphere cannot be pent up in the lower.

This divine hatching method may be seen, too, in the progress of truth, as it unfolds from stage to stage. Nothing is more common than to see a person holding on to a shell in which truth has dwelt, without realizing that the precious thing he wants has gone on and reëmbodied itself in new and living ways which he fails to follow and comprehend. While he is saying in melancholy tones, "They have taken away my Lord and I know not where they have laid him," the living Lord is saying, "Have I been so long time with thee and yet dost thou not know me?"

Truth can no more keep a fixed and permanent form than life can. It lives only by hatching out into higher and ever more adequate expressions of itself, and the old forms in which it lived, the old words through which it uttered itself, become empty and hollow because the warm breath of God has raised the inner life, the spiritual reality, to a higher form of expression.

The writer of the Epistle to the Hebrews was very much impressed with this crumbling of old forms and expressions to give place to the new. God spoke, he says, to our fathers in sundered portions and in a variety of manners, but he is speaking to us now by his Son. The things that can be shaken, he writes, are being removed that the things which cannot be shaken may remain. Luther must have felt this shaking process in his day; and when he saw the old forms of religion crumbling, he wrote that great hymn of the Reformation, "A Mighty Fortress is Our God." He had found something that could not be shaken. He could stand his ground and face the seen and unseen world in faith, because he knew that the hatching was going on, and the new was being born in higher, truer, and more adequate forms as the old was vanishing.

Let us hope that this ancient divine method may still operate in this momentous hour of human history. Never, perhaps, since the fall of Rome, has there been such a world-shaking process affecting every country and all peoples. Immense changes are under way. Nothing will ever be quite the same again. The old is vanishing before our eyes and the new is being born. So much was wrong and outworn, and unjust and inhuman, that the changes must go very far, and they will necessarily involve some breakage. But even now, in this most dynamic period of modern history, that which is to mark permanent progress will come forth, not by a smashing process, but by the hatching of the eggs, by the emergence of the underlying forces of life and the realization of those human hopes and aspirations that have long been held in and suppressed.

There is always the gravest danger from blind rage and sullen wrath. The passionate resentment for the suffering of immemorial wrongs, when once it breaks through the dams of restraint, is an almost irresistible force; but sooner or later the sound, serious sense of the intelligent human race comes into play and brings the world back to order and system. The real gains in these crises are made not by the smashings and the blind iconoclastic blows, but by the wise, clear-sighted fulfillment of the slowly formed ideals which have been the inspiration of many lives before the crisis came. May it be so now! It must not be, it cannot be, that these millions of men shall have unavailingly faced death and mutilation. It was not wreckage and chaos they sought in their brave adventure with death. They went out to build a new world and to destroy, only that a new re-creation might begin. This is the time of incubation and birth, for ripening into reality those mighty hopes that make us men.

It means at once that we must deepen down our lives into the life of God, that we must suppress our petty individual passions and feel the sweep of God's purposes for the new age. In a multitude of ways the world moves on, and as it moves the Spirit of God ends old forms and methods and brings fresh and living ways to light. May we have eyes to see what is of his divine hatching and what is empty shell!

CHAPTER IX
THE MYSTIC'S EXPERIENCE OF GOD

I

The revival of mysticism which has been one of the noteworthy features in the Christianity of our time has presented us with a number of interesting and important questions. We want to know, first of all, what mysticism really is. Secondly, we want to know whether it is a normal or abnormal experience. And omitting many other questions which must wait their turn, we want to know whether mystical experiences actually enlarge our sphere of knowledge, i.e., whether they are trustworthy sources of authentic information and authoritative truth concerning realities which lie beyond the range of human senses.

The answer to the first question appears to be as difficult to accomplish as the return of Ulysses was. The secret is kept in book after book. One can marshall a formidable array of definitions, but they oppose and challenge one another, like the men sprung from the dragon's teeth. For the purposes of the present consideration we can eliminate what is usually included under psychical phenomena, that is, the phenomena of dreams, visions and trances, hysteria and dissociation and esoteric and occult phenomena. Thirty years ago Professor Royce said: "In the Father's house are many mansions, and their furniture is extremely manifold. Astral bodies and palmistry, trances and mental healing, communications from the dead and 'phantasms of the living'—such things are for some people to-day the sole quite unmistakable evidences of the supremacy of the spiritual world." These phenomena are worthy of careful painstaking study and attention, for they will eventually throw much light upon the deep and complex nature of human personality, are in fact already throwing much light upon it. But they furnish us slender data for understanding what is properly meant by mystical experience and its religious and spiritual bearing.

We can, too, leave on one side the metaphysical doctrines which fill a large amount of space in the books of the great mystics. These doctrines had a long historical development and they would have taken essentially the same form if the exponents of them had not been mystics. Mystical experience is confined to no one form of philosophy, though some ways of thinking no doubt favor and other ways retard the experience, as they also often do in the case of religious *faith* in general. Mystical experience, furthermore, must not be confused with what technical expert writers call "the mystic way." There are as many mystical "ways" as there are gates to the New Jerusalem: "On the east three gates, on the north three gates, on the south three gates, and on the west three gates." One might as well try to describe *the way* of making love, or *the way* of appreciating the grand canyon as to describe *the way* to the discovery of God, as though there were only one way.

I am not interested in mysticism as an *ism*. It turns out in most accounts to be a dry and abstract thing, hardly more like the warm and intimate experience than the color of a map is like the country for which it stands. "Canada is very pink," seems quite an inadequate description of the noble country north of our border. It is mystical experience and not mysticism that is worthy of our study. We are concerned with the experience itself, not with second-hand formulations of it. "The mystic," says Professor Royce, "is a thorough-going empiricist;" "God ceases to be an object and becomes an experience," says Professor Pringle-Pattison. If it is an experience we want to find out what happens to the mystic himself inside where he lives. According to those who have been there the experience which we call mystical is charged with the conviction of real, direct contact and commerce with God. It is the almost universal testimony of those who are mystics that they find God through their experience. John Tauler says that in his best moments of "devout prayer and the uplifting of the mind to God," he experiences "the pure presence of God in his own soul," but he adds that all he can tell others about the experience is "as poor and unlike it as the point of a needle is to the heavens above us." "I have met with my God; I have met with my Savior. I have felt the healings drop upon my soul from under His wings," says Isaac Penington in the joy of his first mystical experience. Without needlessly multiplying such testimonies for data, we can say with considerable assurance that mystical experience is consciousness of direct and immediate relationship with some transcendent reality which in the moment of experience is believed to be God. "This is He, this is He," exclaims Isaac Penington, "there is no other: This is He whom I have waited for and sought after from my childhood." Angela of Foligno says that she experienced God, and saw that the whole world was full of God.

II

There are many different degrees of intensity, concentration and conviction in the experiences of different individual mystics, and also in the various experiences of the same individual from time to time. There has been a tendency in most studies of mysticism to regard the state of ecstasy as *par excellence* mystical experience. That is, however, a grave mistake. The calmer, more meditative, less emotional, less ecstatic experiences of God are not less convincing and possess greater constructive value for life and character than do ecstatic experiences which presuppose a peculiar psychical frame and disposition. The seasoned Quaker in the corporate hush and stillness of a silent meeting is far removed from ecstasy, but he is not the less convinced that he is meeting with God. For the *essentia* of mysticism we do not need to insist upon a certain "sacred" mystic way nor upon ecstasy, nor upon any peculiar type of rare psychic upheavals. We do need to insist, however, upon a consciousness of commerce with God amounting to conviction of his presence.

> "Where one heard noise
> And one saw flame,
> I only knew He named my name."

Jacob Boehme calls the experience which came to him, "breaking through the gate," into "a new birth or resurrection from the dead," so that, he says, "I knew God." "I am certain," says Eckhart, "as certain as that I live, that nothing is so near to me as God. God is nearer to me than I am to myself." One of these experiences—the first one—was an ecstasy, and the other, so far as we can tell, was not. It was the flooding in of a moment of God-consciousness in the act of preaching a sermon to the common people of Cologne. The experience of Penington, again, was not an ecstasy; it was the vital surge of fresh life on the first occasion of hearing George Fox preach after a long period of waiting silence. A simple normal case of a mild type is given in a little book of recent date, reprinted from the *Atlantic Monthly*: "After a long time of jangling conflict and inner misery, I one day, *quite quietly and with no conscious effort,* stopped doing the dis-ingenuous thing [I had been doing]. Then the marvel happened. It was as if a great rubber band which had been stretched almost to the breaking point were suddenly released and snapped back to its normal condition. Heaven and earth were changed for me. Everything was glorious because of its relation to some great central life—nothing seemed to matter but that life." Brother Lawrence, a barefooted lay-brother of the seventeenth century, according to the testimony of the brotherhood, attained "an unbroken and undisturbed sense of the Presence of God." He was not an ecstatic; he was a quiet, faithful man who did his ordinary daily tasks with what seemed to his friends "an unclouded vision, an illuminated love and an uninterrupted joy." Simple and humble though he was, he nevertheless acquired, through his experience of God, "an extraordinary spaciousness of mind."

The more normal, expansive mystical experiences come apparently when the personal self is at its best. Its powers and capacities are raised to an unusual unity and fused together. The whole being, with its accumulated submerged life, *finds itself.* The process of preparing for any high achievement is a severe and laborious one, but nothing seems easier in the moment of success than is the accomplishment for which the life has been prepared. There comes to be formed within the person what Aristotle called "a dexterity of soul," so that the person does with ease what he has become skilled to do. Clement of Alexandria called a fully organized and spiritualized person "a harmonized man," that is, adjusted, organized and ready to be a transmissive organ for the revelation of God. Brother Lawrence, who was thus "harmonized," finely says, "The most excellent method which I found of going to God was that of *doing my common business,* purely for the love of God." An earlier mystic of the fourteenth century stated the same principle in these words: "It is my aim to be to the Eternal God what a man's hand is to a man."

There are many human experiences which carry a man up to levels where he has not usually been before and where he finds himself possessed of insight and energies he had hardly suspected were his until that moment. One leaps to his full height when the right inner spring is reached. We are quite familiar with the way in which instinctive tendencies in us and emotions both egoistic and social, become organized under a group of ideas and ideals into a single system which we call a sentiment, such as love, or patriotism, or devotion to truth. It forms slowly and one hardly realizes that it has formed until some occasion unexpectedly brings it into full operation, and we find ourselves able with perfect ease to overcome the most powerful inhibitory and opposing instincts and habits, which, until then, had usually controlled us. We are familiar, too, with the way in which a well-trained and disciplined mind, confronted by a concrete situation, will sometimes—alas not always—in a sudden flash of imaginative insight, discover a universal law revealed there and then in the single phenomenon, as Sir Isaac Newton did and as, in a no less striking way, Sir William Rowan Hamilton did in his discovery of Quaternions. Literary and artistic geniuses supply us with many instances in which, in a sudden flash, the crude material at hand is shot through with vision, and the complicated plot of a drama, the full significance of a character, or the complete glory of a statue stands revealed, as though, to use R. L. Stevenson's illustration, a genie had brought it on a golden tray as a gift from another world. Abraham Lincoln, striking off in a few intense minutes his Gettysburg address, as beautiful in style and perfect in form as anything in human literature, is as good an illustration as we need of the way in which a highly organized person, by a kindling flash, has at his hand all the moral and spiritual gains of a life time.

There is a famous account of the flash of inspiration given by Philo, which can hardly be improved. It is as follows: "I am not ashamed to recount my own experience. At times, when I have proposed to enter upon my wonted task of writing on philosophical doctrines, with an exact knowledge of the materials which were to be put together, I have had to leave off without any work accomplished, finding my mind barren and fruitless, and upbraiding it for its self-complacency, while startled at the might of the Existent One, in whose power it lies to open and close the wombs of the soul. But at other times, when I had come empty, all of a sudden I have been filled with thoughts, showered down and sown upon me unseen from above, so that by Divine possession I have fallen into a rapture and become ignorant of everything, the place, those present, myself, what was spoken or written. For I have received a stream of interpretation, a fruition of light, the most clear-cut sharpness of vision, the most vividly distinct view of the matter before me, such as might be received through the eyes from the most luminous presentation."

The most important mystical experiences are something like that. They occur usually not at the beginning of the religious life but rather in the ripe and developed stage of it. They are the fruit of long-maturing processes. Clement's "the harmonized man" is always a person who has brought his soul into parallelism with divine currents, has habitually practiced his religious insights and has finally formed a unified central self, subtly sensitive, acutely responsive to the Beyond within him. In such experiences which may come suddenly or may come as a more gradual process, the whole self operates and masses all the cumulations of a lifetime. They are no more emotional than they are rational and volitional. We have a total personality, awake, active, and "aware of his life's flow." Instead of seeing in a flash a law of gravitation, or the plot and character of Hamlet, or the uncarven form of Moses the Law-giver in a block of marble, one sees at such times the moral demonstrations of a lifetime and vividly feels the implications that are essentially involved in a spiritual life. In the high moment God is seen to be as sure as the soul is.

> "I stood at Naples once, a night so dark
> I could have scarce conjectured there was earth
> Anywhere, sky or sea or world at all:
> But the night's black was burst through by a blaze—
> Thunder struck blow on blow, earth groaned and bore,
> Through her whole length of mountain visible:
> There lay the city thick and plain with spires,
> And, like a ghost disshrouded, white the sea.
> So may the truth be flashed out by one blow."

To some the truth of God never comes closer than a logical conclusion. He is held to be as a living item in a creed. To the mystic he becomes real in the same sense that experienced beauty is real, or the feel of spring is real, or that summer sunlight is real—he has been found, he has been met, he is present.

Before discussing the crucial question whether these experiences are evidential and are worthy of consideration as an addition to the world's stock of truth and knowledge I must say a few words about the normality or abnormality of them. Nothing of any value can be said on this point of mystical experience in the *abstract*. One must first catch his concrete case.

Some instances are normal and some are undoubtedly abnormal. Trance, ecstasy and rapture are unusual experiences and in that sense not normal occurrences. They usually indicate, furthermore, a pathological condition of personality and are thus abnormal in the more technical sense. There is, however, something more to be said on this point. It seems pretty well established that some persons—and they have often been creative leaders and religious geniuses—have succeeded in organizing their lives, in finding their trail, in charging their whole personality with power, in attaining a moral dynamic and in tapping vast reservoirs of energy by means of states which, if occurring in other persons, would no doubt be called pathological. The real test here is a pragmatic one. It seems hardly sound to call a state abnormal if it has raised the experiencer, as a mystic experience often does, into a hundred horse-power man and through his influence has turned multitudes of other men and women into more joyous, hopeful and efficient persons. This question of abnormality and reality is thus not one to be settled off-hand by a superficial diagnosis.

An experience which brings spaciousness of mind, new interior dimensions, ability to stand the universe—and the people in it—and capacity to work at human tasks with patience, endurance and wisdom may quite intelligently be called normal, though to an external beholder it may look like what he usually calls a trance of hysteria, a state of dissociation, or hypnosis by auto-suggestion. It should be added, however, as I have already said, that mystical experience is not confined to these extremer types. They may or may not be pathological. The calmer and more restrained stages of mysticism are more important and significant and are no more marked with the stigma of hysteria than is love-making, enjoyment of music, devotion to altruistic causes, risking one's life for country, or any lofty experience of *value*.

III

We come at length to the central question of our consideration: Do mystical experiences settle anything? Are they purely subjective and one-sided, or do they prove to have objective reference and so to be two-sided? Do they take the experiencer across the chasm that separates "self" from "Other"? Mystical experience undoubtedly feels as though it had objective reference. It comes to the individual with indubitable authority. He is certain that he has found some thing other than himself. He has an unescapable conviction that he is in contact and commerce with reality beyond the margins of his personal self. "A tremendous muchness is suddenly revealed," as William James once put it.

We do not get very far when we undertake to reduce knowledge to an affair of sense-experience. "They reckon ill who leave me out," can be said by the organized, personal, creative mind as truly as by Brahma. There are many forms of human experience in which the data of the senses are so vastly transcended that they fail to furnish any real explanation of what occurs in consciousness. This is true of all our experiences of *value*, which apparently spring out of synthetic or synoptic activities of the mind, i.e., activities in which the mind is unified and creative. The vibrations of ether which bombard the rods and cones of the retina may be the occasion for the appreciation of beauty in sky or sea or flower, but they are surely not the *cause* of it. The concrete event which confronts me is very likely the occasion for the august pronouncement of moral issues which my conscience makes, but it can not be said that the concrete event in any proper sense *causes* this consciousness of moral obligation. The famous answer of Leibnitz to the crude sense-philosophy of his time is still cogent. To the phrase: "There is nothing in the mind that has not come through the senses," Leibnitz added, "except the mind itself." That means that the creative activity of the mind is always an important factor in experience and one that can not be ignored in any of the processes of knowledge. Unfortunately we have done very little yet in the direction of comprehending the interior depth of the personal mind or of estimating adequately the part which mind itself in its creative capacity plays in all knowledge functions. It will only be when we have succeeded in getting beyond what Plato called the bird-cage theory of knowledge to a sound theory of knowledge and to a solid basis for spiritual values that we shall be able to discuss intelligently the "findings" of the mystic.

The world at the present moment is pitiably "short" in its stock of sound theories of knowledge. The prevailing psychologies do not explain knowledge at all. The behaviorists do not try to explain it any more than the astronomer or the physicist does. The psychologist who reduces mind to an aggregation of describable "mind-states" has started out on a course which makes an explanation forever impossible, since knowledge can be explained only through unity and integral wholeness, never through an aggregation of parts, as though it were a mental "shower of shot." If we expect to talk about *knowledge* and seriously propose to use that great word *truth*, we must at least begin with the assumption of an intelligent, creative, organizing center of self-consciousness which can transcend itself and can *know* what is beyond and other than itself. In short, the talk about a "chasm" between subject and object—knower and thing known—is as absurd as it would be to talk of a chasm between the convex and the concave sides of a curve. Knowledge is always knowledge of an object and mystical experience has all the essential marks of objective reference, as certainly as other forms of experience have.

Professor J. M. Baldwin very well says that there is a form of contemplation in which, as in æsthetic experience, the strands of the mind's diverging dualisms are *"merged and fused."* He adds: "In this experience of a fusion which is not a mixture but which issues in a meaning of its own sort and kind, an experience whose essential character is just this unity of comprehension, consciousness attains its completest, its most direct, and its final apprehension of what Reality is and means." It really comes round to the question whether the mind of a self-conscious person has any way of approach, except by way of the senses, to any kind of reality. There is no *a priori* answer to that question. It can only be settled by experience. It is, therefore, pure dogmatism to say, as Professor Dunlap in his recent attack on mysticism does, that all conscious processes are based on sense-stimulation and all thought as well as perception depends on reaction to sense-stimulus. It is no doubt true that behavior psychology must resort to some such formula, but that only means that such psychology is always dealing with greatly transformed and reduced beings, when it attempts to deal with persons like us who, in the richness of our concrete lives, are never reduced to "behavior-beings." We have interior dimensions and that is the end on't! Some persons—and they are by no means feeble-minded individuals—are as certain that they have commerce with a world within as they are that they have experiences of a world outside in space. Thomas Aquinas, who neither in method nor in doctrine leaned toward mysticism, though he was most certainly "a harmonized man," and who in theory postponed the vision of God to a realm beyond death, nevertheless had an experience two years before he died which made him put his pen and inkhorn on the shelf and never write another word of his *Summa*

Theologiae. When he was reminded of the incomplete state of his great work and was urged to go on with it, he only replied, "I have seen that which makes all that I have written look small to me."

It may be just possible that there is a universe of spiritual reality upon which our finite spirits open inward as inlets open into the sea.

"Like the tides on the crescent sea-beach
When the moon is new and thin
Into our hearts high yearnings
Come welling and surging in;
Come from that mystic ocean
Whose rim no foot has trod.
Some call it longing
But others call it God."

Such a view is perfectly sane and tenable; it conflicts with no proved and demonstrated facts either in the nature of the universe or of mind. It seems anyway to the mystic that there is such a world, that he has found it as surely as Columbus found San Salvador, and that his experience is a truth-telling experience.

IV

But granting that it is truth-telling and has objective reference, is the mystic justified in claiming that he has found and knows God? One does not need to be a very wide and extensive student of mystical experience to discover what a meager stock of knowledge the genuine mystic reports. William James' remarkable experience in the Adirondack woods very well illustrates the type. It had, he says, "an intense significance of some sort, if one could only *tell* the significance.... In point of fact, I can't find a single word for all that significance and don't know what it was significant of, so that it remains a mere boulder of impression."[7] At a later date James refers to that "extraordinary vivacity of man's psychological commerce with something Ideal that *feels as if* it were also actual."[8] The greatest of all the fourteenth century mystics, Meister Eckhart, could not put his *impression* into words or ideas. What he found was a "wilderness of the Godhead where no one is at home," i.e., an Object with no particular differentiated, concrete characteristics. It was not an accident that so many of the mystics hit upon the *via negativa*, the way of negation, or that they called their discovery "the divine Dark."

"Whatever your mind comes at

> I tell you flat
> God is not that."

Mystical experience does not supply concrete information. It does not bring new finite facts, new items that can be used in a description of "the scenery and circumstance" of the realm beyond our sense horizons. It is the awareness of a Presence, the consciousness of a Beyond, the discovery, as James puts it, that "we are continuous with a More of the same quality, which is operative in us and in touch with us."

The most striking effect of such experience is not new fact-knowledge, not new items of empirical information, but new moral energy, heightened conviction, increased caloric quality, enlarged spiritual vision, an unusual radiant power of life. In short, the whole personality, in the case of the constructive mystics, appears to be raised to a new level of life and to have gained from somewhere many calories of life-feeding, spiritual substance. We are quite familiar with the way in which adrenalin suddenly flushes into the physical system and adds a new and incalculable power to brain and muscle. Under its stimulus a man can carry out a piano when the house is on fire. May not, perhaps, some energy from some Source with which our spirits are allied flush our inner being with forces and powers by which we can be fortified to stand the universe and more than stand it! "We are more than conquerors through Him that loved us," is the way one of the world's greatest mystics felt.

Mystical experience—and we must remember as Santayana has said, that "experience is like a shrapnel shell and bursts into a thousand meanings"—does at least one thing. It makes God sure to the person who has had the experience. It raises faith and conviction to the nth power. "The God who said, 'Let light shine out of darkness,' has shined into my heart to give the light of the knowledge of the glory of God," is St. Paul's testimony. "I knew God by revelation," declares George Fox. "I was as one who hath the key and doth open." "The man who has attained this felicity," Plotinus says, "meets some turn of fortune that he would not have chosen, but there is not the slightest lessening of his happiness for that" (En. I: iv. 7). But this experience, with its overwhelming conviction and its dynamic effect, can not be put into the common coin of speech. Frederic Myers has well expressed the difficulty:

"Oh could I tell ye surely would believe it!
   Oh could I only say what I have seen!
How should I tell or how can ye receive it,
   How, till He bringeth you where I have been?"

There is no concrete "information" which can be shared with others.

When Columbus found San Salvador he was able to describe it to those who did not sail with him in the Santa Maria, but when the mystic finds God he can not give us any "knowledge" in plain words of everyday speech. He can only refer to his boulder, or his Gibraltar, of *impression* That situation is what we should expect. We can not, either, describe any of our great emotions. We can not impart what flushes into our consciousness in moments of lofty intuition. We have a submerged life within us which is certainly no less real than our hand or foot. It influences all that we do or say, but we do not find it easy to utter it. In the presence of the sublime we have nothing to say—or if we do say anything it is a great mistake! Language is forged to deal with experiences which are common to many persons, i.e., to experiences which refer to objects in space. We have no vocabulary for the subtle, elusive flashes of vision which are unique, individual and unsharable, as for instance is our personal sense of "the tender grace of a day that is dead." We are forced in all these matters to resort to symbolic suggestion and to artistic devices. Coventry Patmore said with much insight:

"In divinity and love
What's best worth saying can't be said."

I believe that mystical experiences do in the long run expand our knowledge of God and do succeed in verifying themselves. Mysticism is a sort of spiritual protoplasm that underlies, as a basic substance, much that is best in religion, in ethics and in life itself. It has generally been the mystic, the prophet, the seer that has spotted out new ways forward in the jungle of our world, or lifted our race to new spiritual levels. Their experiences have in some way equipped them for unusual tasks, have given supplies of energy to them which their neighbors did not have, and have apparently brought them into vital correspondence with dimensions and regions of reality that others miss. The proof that they have found God, or at least a domain of spiritual reality, does not lie in some new stock of knowledge, not in some gnostic secret, which they bring back; it is to be seen rather in the moral and spiritual fruits which test out and verify the experience.

Consciousness of beauty or of truth or of goodness baffles analysis as much as consciousness of God does. These values have no objective standing ground in current psychology. They are not things in the world of space. They submit to no adequate casual explanation. They have their ground of being in some other kind of world than that of the mechanical order, a world composed of quantitative masses of matter in motion. These experiences of value, which are as real for consciousness as stone walls are, make very clear the fact that there are depths and capacities in the nature of the normal human mind which we do not usually recognize and of which we have scant and imperfect accounts in our text-books. Our minds taken in their full range, in other words, have some sort of contact and relationship with an eternal nature of things far deeper than atoms and molecules. Only very slowly and gradually has the race learned through finite symbols and temporal forms to interpret beauty and truth and goodness which in their essence are as ineffable and indescribable as the mystic's experience of God is. Plato often speaks as though he had high moments of experience when he rose to the naked vision of beauty—beauty "alone, separate and eternal," as he says, and his myths are very likely told, as J. A. Stewart believes, to assist others to experience this same vision—a beauty which "does not grow nor perish, is without increase or diminution and endures for everlasting." But as a matter of fact, however exalted heavenly and enduring beauty may be in its essence we know *what it is* only as it appears in fair forms of objects, of body, of soul, of actions; in harmonious blending of sounds or colors; in well-ordered or happily-combined groupings of many aspects in one unity which is as it ought to be. Truth and moral goodness always transcend our attainments and we sometimes feel that the very end and goal of life is the pursuit of that truth or that goodness which eye hath not seen nor ear heard. But whatever truth we do attain or whatever goodness we do achieve is always concrete. Truth is just this one more added fact that resists all attempts to doubt it. Goodness is just this simple everyday deed that reveals a heroic spirit and a brave venture of faith in the midst of difficulties. So, too, the mystic knowledge of God is not some esoteric communication, supplied through trance or ecstasy; it is an intuitive personal touch with God, felt to be the essentially real, the bursting forth of an intense love for him which heightens all the capacities and activities of life, followed by the slow laboratory results which verify it. "All I could never be" now is. It seems possible to stand the universe—even to do something toward the transformation of it. The bans are read for that most difficult of all marriages, the marriage of the possible with the actual, the ideal with the real. And if the experience does not prove that the soul has found God, it at least does this: it makes the soul feel that proofs of God are wholly unnecessary.

CHAPTER X
PSYCHOLOGY AND THE SPIRITUAL LIFE

I

Twenty years ago in *A Dynamic Faith*, after reviewing the new questions which the great sciences had raised for religion, I said: "There are still harder problems than any of these. Psychology has opened a series of questions which make the boldest tremble for his faith in an endless life or in any spiritual reality." The twenty years that have intervened have made my point much more clear. It is now pretty generally recognized that the deepest issues of the faith are to be settled in this field. The problem of the real nature of the human soul is at the present moment probably the most important religious question before us, for upon the answer to it all our vital spiritual interests depend. If man has no unique interior domain, if he is only a tiny bit of that vast system of naturalism in which every curve of process and development is rigidly determined by antecedent causes, then "spiritual" is only a high-sounding word with a metaphorical significance, but with no basis of reality in the nature of things. There is certainly no "place" in the external world of space where we can expect to find spiritual realities. They are not to be found by going "somewhere." Olympus has been climbed, and it was as naturalistic as any other mountain peak. Eden is only a defined area of Mesopotamia, and that blessed word can work no miracles for us now. The dome of the sky is only an optical illusion. It is no supersensuous realm on which we can build our hopes. The beyond as a spiritual reality is within, or it is nowhere. Psychology, however, has not been very encouraging in promises of hope. It has gone the way of the other sciences and has taken an ever increasing slant toward naturalism. The result is that most so-called "psychologies of religion" reduce religion either to a naturalistic or to a subjective basis, which means in either case that religion as a way to some objective spiritual reality has eluded us and has disappeared as a constructive power. Many a modern psychologist can say with Browning's Cleon:

"And I have written three books on the soul,
Proving absurd all written hitherto,
And putting us to ignorance again."

Two of the main tendencies in what is usually called scientific psychology are (1) the "behaviorist" tendency and (2) the tendency to reduce the inner life to a series of "mind states." Let us consider behaviorism first. This turns psychology into "a purely objective experimental branch of natural science."[9] It aims at "the prediction and control of behavior." "Introspection forms no essential part of its method." One is not concerned with "interpretation in terms of consciousness," one is interested only in reactions, responses—in short, in *behavior* in the presence of stimuli which produce movements. The body is a complicated organ and "mind" is merely a convenient term to express its "activities."[10] The behaviorist "recognizes no dividing line between man and brute." Psychology becomes "the science of behavior,"[11] the study of "the activity of man or animal as it can be observed from the outside, either with or without attempting to determine the mental states by inference from these acts." Emotions become reduced forthwith to "the bodily resonance" set up in the muscular and visceral systems by instinctive movements in the presence of objects, these curious movements being due entirely to the inheritance of physiological structure adapted at least in the early stages to aid survival. There is no way by which behaviorist psychology can give any standing to religion or to any type of spiritual values. "Æsthetics is the study of the useless," as William James baldly states the case. Conscience disappears or becomes another name for the inheritance or acquisition of certain types of social behavior. Everything which we call ethics or morality changes into well-defined and rigidly determined behavior. There is nothing more "spiritual" about it than there is in the fall of a raindrop or in the luminous trail of a meteor, or in any form of what has happily been called "cosmic weather."

This reduction of personality to a center of activity is a reaction from the dualistic sundering of mind and body inherited from Descartes. The theory of psycho-physical parallelism is utterly bankrupt. Idealism, which is an attempt to get round the *impasse* of dualism by treating mind as the only reality, is abhorrent to scientists and unpopular with young philosophers, especially in America. Some other solution is therefore urgent. The easiest one at hand, though it is obviously temporary and superficial, is to cut across the mind loop, ignore its unique, originative, creative capacity and its interior depth, to deal only with body plus body's activities, and to call that "psychology."

The "mind-state" psychology takes us little farther on. It also is a form of naturalism. "Mind-state" psychology makes more of introspection than behaviorist psychology does, and it works more than the latter does in terms of consciousness, which for the behaviorist can be almost ignored or questioned as an existing reality. According to this view, mind or consciousness is composed of a vast number of "elemental units," and the business of psychology is to analyze and describe these units or states and to discover the laws of their arrangement or succession. Mind, on this theory, is an aggregate or sum total of "states." Professor James, who gives great place to "mind states," will, however, not admit that they are permanent and repeatable "units," passing and returning unaltered. In his usual vivid way he says that "a permanently existing 'idea' [i.e., mental unit] which makes its appearance before the footlights of consciousness at periodical intervals is as mythological an entity as the Jack of Spades."[12] And yet he continues to deal with mind as a vast series of more or less describable states. Some states are "substantive," such as our "perceptions," our "memories," or our definite "images," when the mind perches and rests upon some clear and describable thought, and on the other hand there are "transitive states" which are vague, hard to catch or hold or express, and which reveal the mind in flight, in passage, on the way from one substantive state to another.

When we ask the "mind-state" psychologist to tell us about the soul or to supply us with a working substitute for it, he relegates it to the scrap heap where lie the collected rubbish and the antiquated mental furniture of the medieval centuries. We have no need of it. It is only a *word* anyhow. It has always been an expensive luxury and a continual bother. We are better off with it gone. When we look about for a "self as knower," or for a guardian of our identity, we find all that we need in these same "passing states of consciousness." They not only know things and facts, but they also know themselves, and successively inherit and adapt all the preceding "states" have gained and acquired. The state of the present moment owns the thoughts and experiences which preceded it, for "what possesses the possessor possesses the possessed." "In our waking hours," Professor James says, "though each pulse of consciousness dies away and is replaced by another, yet that other, among the things it knows, knows its own predecessor and finding it 'warm,' greets it saying, 'Thou art *mine* and part of the same self with me.'" It seems, then, this famous writer concludes, that "states of consciousness are all that psychology needs to do her work with. Metaphysics or theology may prove the soul to exist; but for psychology the hypothesis of such a substantial principle of unity is superfluous."[13] We are certainly hard up if we must depend on proofs which theology can give us!

We are thus once more reduced to a condition of sheer naturalism. Our stream of consciousness is only a rapid succession of passing states, each "state" causally attached to a molecular process in the brain. "Every *psychosis* is the result of a *neurosis*." There is no soul, there is no creative spiritual pilot of the stream, there is no freedom, there are no moral values, there is nothing but passing "cosmic weather," sometimes peeps of sunshine, sometimes moonshine, sometimes drizzle or blizzard, and sometimes cyclone or waterspout! To meet the appalling thinness of this "cinema" of mind states, we are given the comfort of believing that there is an under-threshold world within, possibly more real and surely more important than this little rivulet of states which make up our conscious life. There is a "fringe" to consciousness more wonderful than that which adorned the robe of the high priest. This "fringe" defies description and baffles all analysis. It is a halo or penumbra which surrounds every "state" and holds all the states vitally together, so that "states" turn out to be unsundered in some deeper mysterious currents of being. Others would call this same underlying, mysterious part of us the subliminal "self," i.e., under-threshold "self." It is a kind of semi-spiritual matrix where the states of consciousness are formed and gestated. It is the source to which we may trace everything that can not be explained by the avenues of the senses. Demons and divinities knock at its doors and visitants from superterrestrial shores peep in at its windows. It is often treated, especially of course by Frederic Myers, as a deeper "self," more or less discontinuous with our conscious upper self, the self of mind states. All work of genius is due to "subliminal uprushes," "an emergence into the current of ideas which the man is consciously manipulating of other ideas which he has not consciously originated, but which have shaped themselves beyond his will in profounder regions of his being." As is well known, Professor James resorts to these "subliminal uprushes" for his explanation of all the deeper religious experiences and he has done much to give credit to these "profounder regions of our being" and to make the subliminal theory popular. He does not, however, as Myers does, treat it as another "self," an intermediary between earth and heaven, a messenger and a mediator of all those higher and diviner aspects of life which transcend the sphere of sense and of the empirical world.

II

No theory certainly is sound which begins by cutting the subconscious and the conscious life apart into two more or less dissociated selves. There is every indication and evidence of continuity and correlation between what is above and what is below the threshold which in any case is as relative and artificial a line as is the horizon. The so-called "uprushes" of the genius are finely correlated with his normal experience into which they "uprush." The "uprushes" which convey truth to Socrates beautifully fit, first, the character of the man and, secondly, the demands of the temporal environment. Dante's "uprushes" correspond to the psychological climate of the medieval world, and Shakespeare's "uprushes" are well suited to the later period of the Renaissance. All subliminal communications are congruent and consonant with the experience of the person who receives them. The visions of apocalyptic seers are all couched in the imagery of the apocalyptic schools, and so, too, the reports of mediums are all in terms of spiritualistic beliefs. We shall never find the solution of our religious problems by dividing the inner life of man into two unrelated selves, by whatever name we call them, for any religion that is to be real must go all the way through us, must unify all our powers, and must furnish a spring and power by which we live here and now in the sphere of our consciousness, our character, and our will.

It proves to be just as impossible to cut consciousness up into the fragmentary bits or units called mind states, or to sunder it into a so-called "self as knower" and "self as known." Consciousness is never a shower of shot—a series of discontinuous units. It is the most completely integral unity known to us anywhere in the universe. There are no "parts" to it; it is without breaks or gaps. It is one undivided whole. The only unit we can properly talk about is our unique persisting personal self in conscious relation to an environment. We can, of course, treat consciousness in the abstract as an aggregate of states and we can formulate a scientific account of this constructed entity as we can of any other abstracted section of reality. But this abstracted entity is forever totally different from the warm and intimate inner life within us, as we actually live it and feel its flow. Any state or process which we may talk about is only an artificial fragment of a larger, deeper reality which gives the "fragment" its peculiar being and makes it what it is. Underneath all that appears and happens in the conscious flow is the personal self for whom the appearances occur. Any psychologist who explicitly leaves this out of his account always implicitly smuggles it in again.

The most striking fact of experience is *knowing that we know*. The same consciousness which knows any given object in the same pulse of consciousness knows itself as knowing it. Self-consciousness is present in all consciousness of objects. The thinker that thinks is involved in and is bound up with all knowledge, even of the simplest sort. Every idea, every feeling, and every act of will is what it is because it is in living unity with our entire personal self. If any such "state" got dissociated, slipped away and undertook to do business on its own hook, it would be as unknown to us as our guardian angel is. The mind that knows can never be separated from the world that is known. One can think in abstraction of a mind apart by itself and of a world equally isolated—but no such mind and no such world actually exist. To be a real mind, a real self, is to be in active commerce with a real world given in experience. One thinks his object in the same unified pulse of consciousness in which he thinks himself and vice versa. There is no self-consciousness without object-consciousness, and there is no object-consciousness without self-consciousness. Outer and inner, knower and known, are not two but forever one. The "soul," therefore, is not something hidden away in behind or above and beyond our ideas and feelings and will activities. It is the active living unity of personal consciousness—the one psychic integer and unit for a true psychology. It binds all the items of experience into one indivisible unity, one organic whole through which our personal type of life is made possible. At every moment of waking, intelligent life we look out upon each fact, each event, each experience from a wider self which organizes the new fact in with its former experiences, weaves it into the web of its memories and emotions and purposes, makes the new fact a part of itself, and yet at the same time knows itself as transcending and outliving the momentary fact.

When we study the personal self deeply enough, not as cut up into artificial units, but as the living, undivided whole, which is implied in all coherent experience, we find at once a basis for those ideal values that are rightly called spiritual and for "those mighty hopes that make us men." The first step toward a genuine basis of spiritual life is to be found in the restoration of the personal self to its true place as the ultimate fact, or datum, of self-conscious experience. As soon as we come back to this central reality, our unified, unique, self-active personality, we find ourselves in possession of material enough; as Browning would say,

> "For fifty hopes and fears
> As old and new at once as nature's self,
> To rap and knock and enter in our soul,
> Take hands and dance there, a fantastic ring,
> Round the ancient idol, on his base again,—
> The grand Perhaps!"

What we find at once, even without a resort to a subliminal self, or to "uprushes," is that our normal, personal self-consciousness is a unique, living, self-active, creative center of energies, dealing not only with space and time and tangible things, but dealing as well with realities which are space- and time-transcending. "The things that are not" prove to be immense factors in our lives and constantly "bring to naught the things that are." The greatest events of history have not been due to physical forces; they have been due to plans and ideals which were real only in the viewless minds of men. What *was not yet* brought about what was to be. Alexander the Great with his physical forces, sweeping across the ancient world like a cataclysm of nature, was certainly no more truly a world-builder than was Jesus, who had no armies, who used no tangible forces, but merely put into operation those "things that were not," i.e., his ideas of what ought to be and his conviction that love is stronger than Roman legions. The simplest and humblest of us, like the Psalmist, find the Meshech where we sojourn too straitened and narrow for us. We have all cried, "Woe is me that I sojourn in Meshech!" The reason that we discover the limits and bounds of our poor Meshech is that we are all the time going beyond the hampering Meshech that tries to contain and imprison us.

The thing which spoils all our finite camping places is our unstilled consciousness that we are made for something more than we have yet realized or attained. Our ideals are an unmistakable intimation of our time-transcending nature. We can no more stop with *that which is* than Niagara can stop at the fringe of the fall. All consciousness of the higher rational type is continually carried forward toward the larger whole that would complete and fulfill its present experience. We are aware of the limit only because we are already beyond it. The present is a pledge of more; the little arc which we have gives us a ground of faith in the full circle which we seek. A study of man's life which does not deal with this inherent idealizing tendency is like *Hamlet* with Hamlet left out. Martineau declared:

> "Amid all the sickly talk about 'ideals' which has become the commonplace of our age, it is well to remember that so long as they are dreams of future possibility and not faiths in present realities, so long as they are a mere self-painting of the yearning spirit and not its personal surrender to immediate communion with an infinite Perfection, they have no more solidity or steadiness than floating air-bubbles, gay in the sunshine and broken by the passing wind.... The very gate of entrance to religion, the moment of its new birth, is the discovery that your ideal is the everlasting Real, no transient brush of a fancied angel wing, but the abiding presence and persuasion of the Soul of souls."[14]

In the same vein Pringle-Pattison, one of the wisest of our living teachers, has said:

> "Consciousness of imperfection, the capacity for progress, and the pursuit of perfection, are alike possible to man only through the universal life of thought and goodness in which he shares and which, at once an indwelling presence and an unattainable ideal, draws him 'on and always on.'"[15]

It is here in these experiences of ours which spring out of our real nature, but which always carry us beyond *what is* and which make it impossible for us to live in a world composed of "things," no matter how golden they are, that we have the source of our spiritual values. When we talk about values we may use the word in two senses. In the ordinary sense we mean something extrinsic, utilitarian. We mean that we possess something which can be exchanged for something else. It is precious because we can sell it or swap it or use it to keep life going. In the other sense we see value in reference to something which *ought to be*, whether it now is or not. It is *fit* to be, it would justify its being in relation to the whole reality. When we speak of ethical or spiritual values we are thinking of something that will minister to the highest good of persons or of a society of persons. Value in this loftier meaning always has to do with ideals. A being without any conscious end or goal, i.e., without an ideal, would have no sense of worth, no spiritual values. It does not appear on the level of instinct. It arises as an appreciation of what ought to be realized in order to complete and fulfill any life which is to be called good. Obviously a person with rich and complex interests will have many scales of value, but lower and lesser ones will fall into place under wider and higher ones, so that one forms a kind of hierarchical system of values with some overtopping end of supreme worth dominating the will.

It becomes one of the deepest questions in the world what connection there is between man's spiritual values or ideals and the eternal nature of things in the universe. Are these ideals of ours, these values which seem to raise us from the naturalistic to the spiritual level, just our subjective creations, or are they expressions of a coöperating and rational power beyond us and yet in us, giving us intimations of what is true and best in a world more real than that of matter and motion? These ideal values, such as our appreciation of beauty, our confidence in truth, our dedication to moral causes, our love for worthy persons, our loyalty to the Kingdom of God, are not born of selfish preference or individual desire. They are not capricious like dreams and visions. They attach to something deeper than our personal wishes, in fact our faith in them and our devotion to them often cause us to take lines of action straight against our personal wishes and our individual desires. They stand the test of stress and strain, they weather the storms of time which submerge most things, they survive all shock and mutations and only increase in worth with the wastage of secondary goods. They rest on no mere temporary impulse or sporadic whim. They have their roots deep in the life of the race. They have lasted better than Andes or Ararat, and they are based upon common, universal aspects of rational life. They are at least as sure and prophetic as are laws of triangles and relations of space. If we can count on the permanence of the multiplication table and on the continuity of nature, no less can we count on the conservation of values and the continued significance of life.

They seem thus to belong to the system of the universe and to have the guardianship of some invisible Pilot of the cosmic ship. The streams of moral power and the spiritual energies that have their rise in good persons are as much to be respected facts of the universe as are the rivers that carry ships of commerce. Moral goodness is a factor in the constitution of the world, and the eternal nature of the universe backs it as surely as it backs the laws of hydrogen. It does not back every ideal, for some ideals are unfit and do not minister to a coherent and rationally ordered scheme of life. Those ideals only have the august sanction and right of way which are born out of the age-long spiritual travail of the race and which tend to organize men for better team efforts, i.e., which promote the social community life, the organism of the Spirit. Through these spiritual forces, revealed in normal ethical persons, we are, I believe, nearer to the life of God and closer to the revealing centers of the universe than we are when we turn to the subliminal selves of hysterics. The normal interior life of man is boundless and bottomless. It is not a physical reality, to be measured by foot rules or yardsticks. It is a reality of a wholly different order. It is essentially spiritual, i.e., of spirit. In its organized and differentiated life this personal self of ours is often weak and erratic. We feel the *urge* which belongs to the very nature of *spirit*, but we blunder in our direction, we bungle our aims and purposes, we fail to discover what it is that we really want. But we are never insulated from the wider spiritual environment which constitutes the true inner world from which we have come and to which we belong. There are many ways of correspondence with this environment. No way, however, is more vital, more life-giving than this way of dedication to the advancement of the moral ideals of the world.

www.ingramcontent.com/pod-product-compliance
Lightning Source LLC
Chambersburg PA
CBHW081622100526
44590CB00021B/3550